THE
FREER
GALLERY
OF
ART

FREER GALLERY OF ART

Contents

CHINESE SCULPTURE GALLERY

THE FREER GALLERY OF ART

I China

Compiled by The Freer Gallery of Art

Washington, D.C.

Produced by Kodansha Ltd.
Tokyo, Japan

Published by KODANSHA, LTD., 2–12–21 Otowa, Bunkyo-ku, Tokyo, Japan.

Printed in Japan.

Library of Congress Catalog Card No. 72–154732.

CHARLES LANG FREER

CHARLES LANG FREER MEMORIAL AT THE KOETSU TEMPLE, KYOTO

Preface

THE FREER GALLERY of Art came into being when Charles Lang Freer, of Detroit, gave his collection in trust to the Smithsonian Institution, provided funds for a building to house it, and established an endowment the income from which would make possible the purchase of additional works of Oriental art and finance a program of research into the civilizations of the East.

The formal deed of gift was executed on May 5, 1906, during the administration of President Theodore Roosevelt. Under the terms of this deed, Mr. Freer retained the right to keep the collection in his possession during his lifetime and to make additions to it, although it was understood that an object once incorporated in the collection should not be removed from it. After his death the collection was to be removed to Washington and placed in a building given by the founder, designed in accordance with his wishes and erected within the grounds of the Smithsonian Institution. In accepting this gift, the Regents of the Smithsonian Institution agreed to care for and maintain the building and collections at public expense.

Charles Freer was born at Kingston, N. Y. on February 25, 1856. His ancestors were French Huguenots who fled France during the religious persecutions of the 17th century; and the first member of the family to come to America was one of the original holders of a royal land grant in New Paltz, New York.

As a boy of 14, after having attended public school, he went to work in a cement factory in his neighborhood. At 16 he was a clerk in the general store of John C. Brodhead at Kingston. In the same building with the store were the offices of the New York, Kingston & Syracuse Railroad of which Col. Frank J. Hecker was the superintendent. The latter was attracted by the ability of young Freer and in 1873 took him into his employ, thus beginning an association that was to endure for life. After several years of railroad work Charles Freer went with Colonel Hecker to Detroit, where, in 1880, he took part in the organization of the Peninsular Car Works and became assistant treasurer. Between 1880 and 1900 Mr. Freer was associated with this company and those which succeeded it. In 1900, after completing his work in the mergers that formed the American Car & Foundry Co., he retired from active business. He was 44 years old.

For the last 19 years of his life, Mr. Freer devoted the greater part of his time and interest to the study and development of his art collections, begun during the early eighties.

His first acquistitions were etchings and lithographs. Among the earliest objects in the present collection is the set of Whistler etchings, "Venice, Second Series," bought in 1887.

About 1888, on a visit to England he met James Abbott McNeill Whistler, and from this moment he turned more and more to the art of Japan. A brief period of interest in the Ukiyo-e prints led him to the older arts of Japan—paintings, screens, and pottery—and these in turn directed his interest to the classic arts of China.

Mr. Freer made four trips to the Far East: in 1895, 1907, 1909 and 1910/11. It was during these trips that he studied public and private collections, discussed problems with scholars and collectors, and made purchases that would improve and expand his own collections. Entries in his diaries and statements from his correspondence from these years reveal how much Mr. Freer learned during these trips, and how modest he was about his own knowledge, even after he was acknowledged as an important collector.

His first trip to China in 1895, when he was thirty-nine years old, was actually an unexpected stop enroute to Japan. Mr. Freer stopped briefly in Hong Kong for three days and visited Shanghai for a week before sailing for Japan where he traveled extensively for almost four months. While he had not planned to visit China at this time, he evidently enjoyed his brief glimpse of that country. Entries in his diarly made during this first trip are extremely terse, suggesting that he was still weighing his reactions to the new and exciting surroundings. It was on his arrival in Japan in late April of 1895 that Mr. Freer, through a series of coincidences, met the great silk exporter and art collector, Mr. Tomitaro Hara; and he became subsequently a frequent visitor at Mr. Hara's villa in the suburbs of Yokohama and was able to study the many masterpieces in his collection. Mr. Hara, in turn, introduced Mr. Freer to another famous collector, Mr. T. Masuda, head of the great international banking firm of Mitsui. So from the very outset, Mr. Freer had the advantage of the intimate friendship of two of the greatest collectors in Japan; and it was under their guidance that he began to develop his knowledge and taste in the field of Far Eastern art, and to start building up his own collection.

When he visited China again twelve years later, in 1907, he was already well-known. Yet he humbly acknowledged his need for further study, and referred to his trip as being made specifically for research. Once again, his stay in China was brief. He arrived in Hong Kong on Easter Sunday, March 31. After buying several pieces of Chinese ceramics he left for Canton on April 2 where he made some additional purchases. This was his first trip inland, and the old walled city of Canton, a sharp contrast to the more Western flavor of Hong Kong and Shanghai, made a favorable impression on him. Returning to Hong Kong, he made some additional purchases of pottery and bronzes before leaving for Shanghai. During his three-day stay in Shanghai, he still found time to acquire several objects before sailing for Japan.

So well-known had Mr. Freer and his collections become during the twelve years between his first and second visit to Japan, that all collections in Japan were opened to him. He records with obvious satisfaction that he was able to see practically all the early Chinese paintings owned publicly and privately in Japan.

Two years later, in 1909, Mr. Freer was in Hong Kong again. He stayed at the German Consul-General's home situated just below the peak, affording a superb view of the harbor. The Consul-General, who also was interested in Chinese antiquities, had arranged for experts, collectors and dealers from Canton and Hong Kong to meet Mr. Freer. The two men spent long days in study before Mr. Freer went to Shanghai whence, after a brief stop, he sailed to Ch'ing-tao, an important German concession in Shantung province, enroute to Peking via Tientsin. During a subsequent visit to Tientsin, he saw the collection of the great Manchu statesman, Tuan-fang, and described it as the best he had ever seen and Tuan-fang as the keenest and ablest collector he had ever met.

In Peking Mr. Freer saw the most famous monuments, including the Temples of Heaven and Agriculture and the Drum Temple. Reluctantly he became part of the busy social life of the capital. There was still time for purchases, however, and in an effort to keep the full extent of them private, he rented several rooms in the Tartar City and transacted all of his business there. He was delighted to find that the Chinese dealers thought he was the buyer for some American auction house. The bustle of the Tartar City appealed to Mr. Freer, and he compared it with the bazaars of Cairo and Constantinople. In trips taken outside the city, he went to see the Summer Palace, the Great Wall and the Ming tombs.

During the four and one-half weeks spent in Peking Mr. Freer amassed a large collection of bronzes, ceramics and paintings. Before leaving the city, he arranged for eight crates of art objects to be shipped to his home in Detroit. He noted proudly that these purchases brought his Chinese collection up to the level of his Japanese and Persian collections. The success of his first visit to the capital of China induced Mr. Freer to make a second trip the following year.

The most memorable of Mr. Freer's visits to China was his last, made in 1910 and 1911. His diaries and letters from this trip are filled with the names of dealers and collectors, as well as some of the most famous connoisseurs of the period, including Friedrich Hirth, John C. Ferguson, Langdon Warner and A. W. Bahr. These days were filled with work and study. In a few terse words Mr. Freer records that he arrived in Shanghai from Nagasaki on September 11, 1910, and looked at Chinese ceramics and paintings the same day. Three days later he sailed for Ch'ing-tao, and by the 21st of the month was once again in Peking. With his usual good fortune, Mr. Freer was able to join the official party of the visiting American Secretary of War and his wife, and thereby gained entrance to the confines of the Forbidden City. Again he visited Tuan-fang in Tientsin and saw additional items in that famous collection.

The most important part of this last visit to China was the journey to the interior. Originally Mr. Freer had planned a trip which would enable him to see three ancient capitals: K'ai-feng, Loyang and Ch'ang-an. On the 29th of October he went by train to Chang-te Fu and reached K'ai-feng the following day. The temples and palaces of the ancient city completely captivated Mr. Freer. He described K'ai-feng as being to him what Hōryūji had been to Ernest Fenollosa. In a side trip, he went to see the famous rock-cut temples of Kung-hsien.

The most difficult and dangerous part of the journey was to the Buddhist rock-cut caves on the I River at Lung-men near Lo-yang in Honan province. Lung-men never was very safe because its many caves provided hiding places for brigands who preyed on the heavy traffic that passed through the gorge of the river. Officials and friends warned Mr. Freer of the dangers involved in such a trip.

Before leaving for Lung-men, Mr. Freer consulted with the Lieutenant Governor of the province, who, acting under instructions from the Chinese government in Peking, stipulated that six soldiers would accompany Mr. Freer and his party, which already included a cook, a photographer, a servant, and an interpreter. The concern of the Chinese government for the safety of such a distinguished visitor became apparent when Mr. Freer arrived at the site. He was amused to find that he always was accompanied by at least four soldiers. Later, the official of the district assigned several of his own guard to patrol the area, shooting rifles to frighten away bandits. The constant sound of rifle fire did little to alleviate the fears of the other people in Mr. Freer's party. In his diary he writes, "Enroute here my photographer was stoned and received one ugly blow over his right eye, but Pond's Extract put him back in harness again today, although the dropping of a pin now startles him. My cook sleeps with the new bread knife I bought in Peking, my interpreter wraps countless blankets around him when he lies down, the photographer never sleeps, my servant wept last night when the temple cat mewed outside; so if the brigands overpower the guard, I shall dive under my folding cot."

In spite of the difficulties encountered, Mr. Freer and his staff worked long hours each day, and took a large number of photographs of the various caves and sculptures that are found in the cliffs on both sides of the river at Lung-men. These photographs, which are in the study collection of the Freer Gallery, provide an important record of the site for students of Chinese Buddhist sculpture.

His work at Lung-men completed, Mr. Freer was given an elegant banquet at the yamen by the official of Honan-fu. He had hoped to visit the Buddhist rock-cut caves at Yün-kang in Shansi province, but his staff had had enough and they all refused to go further. Flooding prevented any attempt to visit Ch'ang-an so Mr. Freer and his dispirited party returned to Peking.

Back in the capital, his time was occupied with purchasing ceramics, bronzes and paintings. On December 21 he left Peking for Mukden to visit the palace collections. After spending the Christmas holidays in the rather bleak surroundings of the northern city, he traveled to Dairen and Port Arthur, before sailing for Shanghai.

In Shanghai he saw the famous collection owned by P'ang Yüan-chi, and made several purchases from him. One of these purchases is the handscroll entitled, "Ch'en Yüan-ta Admonishing Liu Ts'ung", an especially important example of Chinese figure painting in the Freer Gallery.

After the long weeks of travel and collecting, Mr. Freer decided to take a pleasure trip to Hangchow with several friends. They arranged to sail on two houseboats named "Annie" and "Lois", which were towed by a steam tug on the river and canal route from Shanghai to Hangchow. Entries in his diary and statements in his letters record Mr. Freer's excitement with the city and his appreciation of the beauties of the West Lake and surrounding area. This was a fitting climax to the longest and last trip Mr. Freer was to make to China.

He returned to Shanghai by train and sailed for Nagasaki on February 20, 1911. The intensity of his research during this trip is attested by the long entries found at the end of his diaries for 1910 and 1911. Extensive notes record the special features and kiln sites of the most famous Chinese wares. His attempts to learn some rudiments of spoken Chinese can also be found in the notes on pronunciation of basic Chinese phrases. Once he had returned to the United States, the cataloguing of his collection and a series of illnesses prevented Mr. Freer from returning to the Far East again. But the results of his four trips can be seen in the growing discernment that characterized his purchases during the years remaining before his death in 1919.

As a collector, Charles Freer possessed a sensitive and discriminating taste that stood him in good stead as he adventured among the fine arts of the classic antiquity of China, just beginning to be seen by Western eyes. His generous provision for future acquisitions and for serious study in this field was significant of his recognition of its importance to scholarship as well as to aesthetics. His gift was appropriately placed in the care of the Smithsonian Institution, whose seal is inscribed with the words: "For the increase and diffusion of knowledge among men." Mr. Freer died in New York City on September 25, 1919.

The reason for the establishment of the Freer Gallery of Art was Mr. Freer's desire to make his important collections available to the people of the United States, and to encourage and promote continuing research into the civilizations of those countries in which the Oriental objects were created.

The two principal provisions of his will provide for additions to the Oriental collections and for the study of their sources. Though Mr. Freer was not a scholar himself, he had a deep and sincere regard for truth, and for exact understanding of the fine arts; and his generous provision for acquisition and study in the Oriental field was significant of his recognition of the importance of scholarship, as well as of the improvement of aesthetic standards.

The implementation of the very general terms of the will was left largely to the imagination and initiative of the first Director (or Curator, as he was then called), John Ellerton Lodge. Following Mr. Freer's death, the building was completed and the collections were moved from Detroit to Washington; installation and the arrangement of storage facilities were carried on during 1921 and 1922 and the building was formally opened on May 2, 1923. From the very beginning important additions were made to the collection under the terms set forth in Mr. Freer's will. With the passing of the years and the steady increase in interest and knowledge, the quality and importance of the works of Far Eastern and Near Eastern art that have come on the market have become higher and higher so that the purchases of the last four decades have not only augmented the size of the collections but have raised the level of quality to new heights. It is no exaggeration to say that wherever the arts of Asia are collected or studied today, the collections of the Freer Gallery are recognized as setting a standard of excellence by which other collections and individual objects may be judged. Mr. Freer bequeathed some 9,000 objects to the nation; and in the intervening years almost 2,000 more have been added to the collections. For reasons of physical space and, even more important, to maintain a tasteful installation, only a small percentage of the collection is exhibited at any one time; but the objects on exhibition are changed now and then, and objects in storage are always available by appointment to students and any others with special interests. This point was stressed by Mr. Freer in the first paragraph of the Deed of Gift when he said, "the building shall be constructed and equipped by the said Institution with the sum so bequeathed with special regard for the convenience of students and others desirous of an opportunity for uninterrupted study of the objects embraced thereunder." Occasional special exhibitions are held to illustrate particular aspects of Oriental art, and these are made up of objects in the collection. The Deed of Gift specifically forbids loans to or from the collection.

The technical laboratory, established at the Gallery in 1951, carries on a program of research into the methods and materials of ancient craftsmen with the twofold goal of increasing our knowledge of the history of technology in Asia and enabling the Gallery to better preserve and potect the objects of art with which it is entrusted.

And so the Freer Gallery of Art stands on the Mall in Washington today as a monument to the ideals of that remarkable man, Charles Lang Freer. The Oriental collections continue to grow, broadening in scope and improving in quality; and the research of the scholarly staff continues to throw new light on the spiritual, historical, and physical origins of the works of art. Successive directors of the Gallery have striven to carry on this program on the same high level of excellence as that on which it was established by the founder.

JOHN A. POPE
Director, The Freer Gallery of Art

I

青銅器・玉器
BRONZE AND JADE

1
觚　殷時代
KU　SHANG DYNASTY

2
壷　殷時代
HU　SHANG DYNASTY

KU'ANG   SHANG DYNASTY

4

人面蛇身盉　殷時代中頃

HUO　　　MIDDLE SHANG DYNASTY

5
盉　　殷時代
HUO　　SHANG DYNASTY

6
卣　殷時代
YU　SHANG DYNASTY

7

觥　　周時代初め

KUANG　　EARLY CHOU DYNASTY

8
簋　周時代初め
KUEI　EARLY CHOU DYNASTY

9

方彝　周時代初め

FANG-I　EARLY CHOU DYNASTY

10
虎像　　周時代
TIGER　　CHOU DYNASTY

11
手品師　周時代
JUGGLER　CHOU DYNASTY

12

銀象嵌菱紋扁壺　　周時代末

PIEN-HU　　LATE CHOU DYNASTY

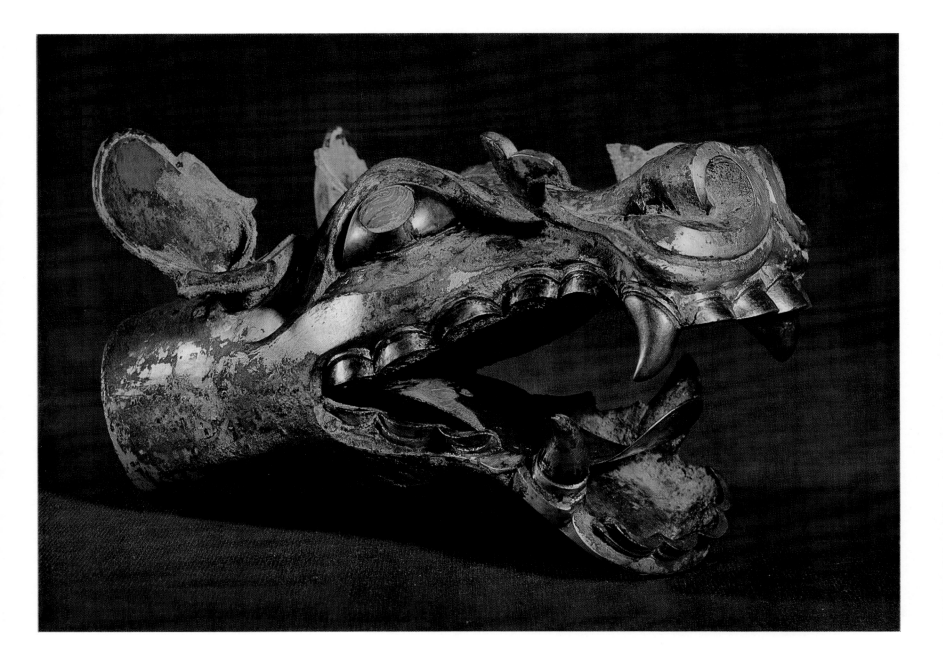

先端装飾　　　　　周時代
TERMINAL ORNAMENT　CHOU DYNASTY

14

博山香炉　　　周時代末—漢時代初め

INCENSE BURNER, PO-SHAN HSIANG-LU　　　LATE CHOU—EARLY HAN DYNASTY

15
玉戚　　　　　　　　殷時代
JADE BATTLE-AXE PI DISC　　SHANG DYNASTY

16
トルコ石象嵌・青銅玉製戈　　殷時代
BRONZE AND JADE KO　　　SHANG DYNASTY

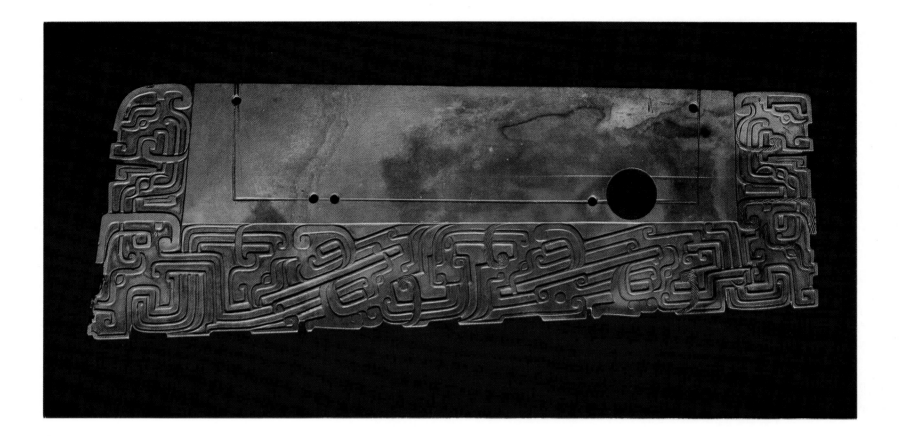

17
玉笏　　　　　　　　　周時代
JADE CEREMONIAL BLADE, HU　CHOU DYNASTY

18
佩玉　　　　　　　　　周時代
JADE PLAQUE　　CHOU DYNASTY

19
佩玉　　　　周時代
JADE NECKLACE　　CHOU DYNASTY

20
玉盦　　　　　　周時代
JADE COVERED CUP　　CHOU DYNASTY

21
帯鉤　　　周時代
BELT HOOK　　CHOU DYNASTY

22
帯鉤　　　周時代
BELT HOOK　　CHOU DYNASTY

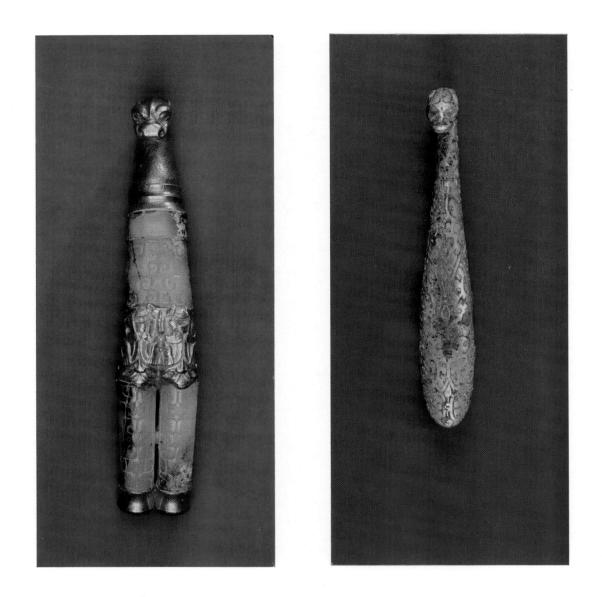

23
帯鉤　　　周時代
BELT HOOK　　CHOU DYNASTY

24
帯鉤　　　周時代
BELT HOOK　　CHOU DYNASTY

25
青銅鏡　　　周時代
BRONZE MIRROR　　CHOU DYNASTY

26
青銅鏡　　　唐時代
BRONZE MIRROR　　T'ANG DYNASTY

27
青銅鏡　　　唐時代
BRONZE MIRROR　　T'ANG DYNASTY

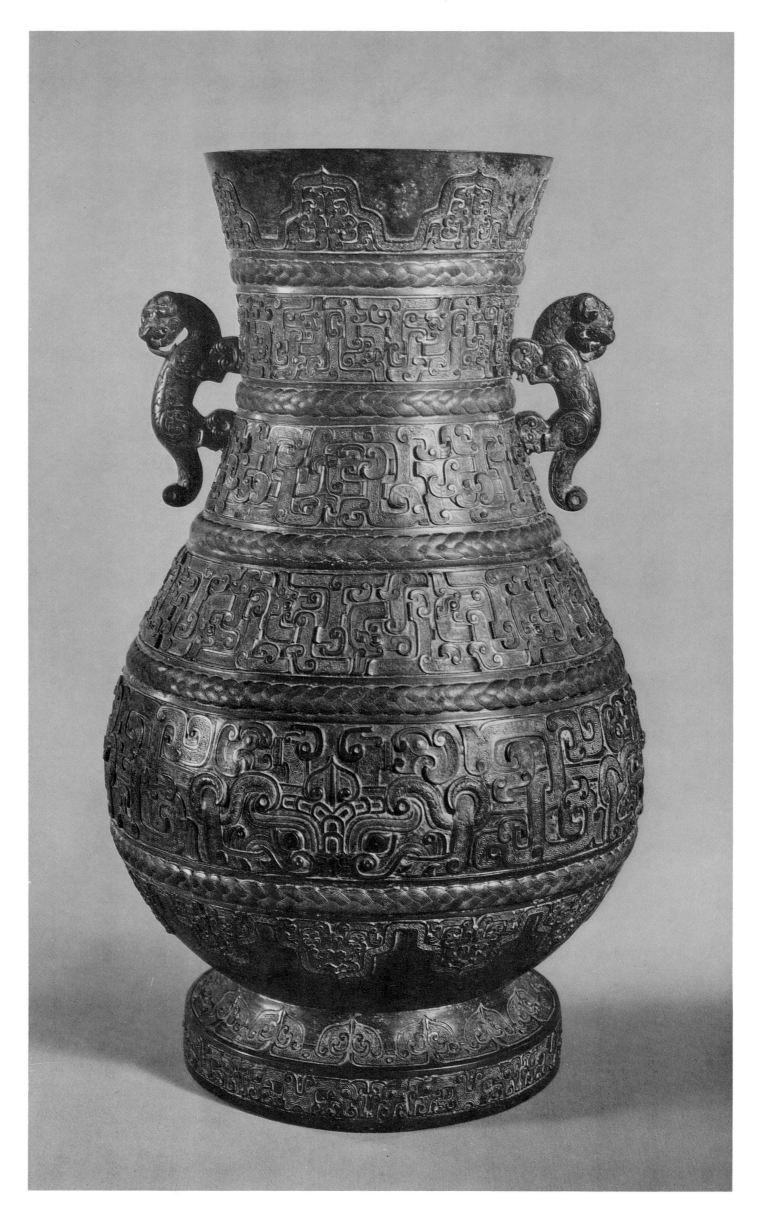

28
壺　周時代末
HU　LATE CHOU DYNASTY

29
鑑　周時代末
CHIEN　LATE CHOU DYNASTY

30

豆　周時代末
TOU　LATE CHOU DYNASTY

31

奩　漢時代

LIEN　　HAN DYNASTY

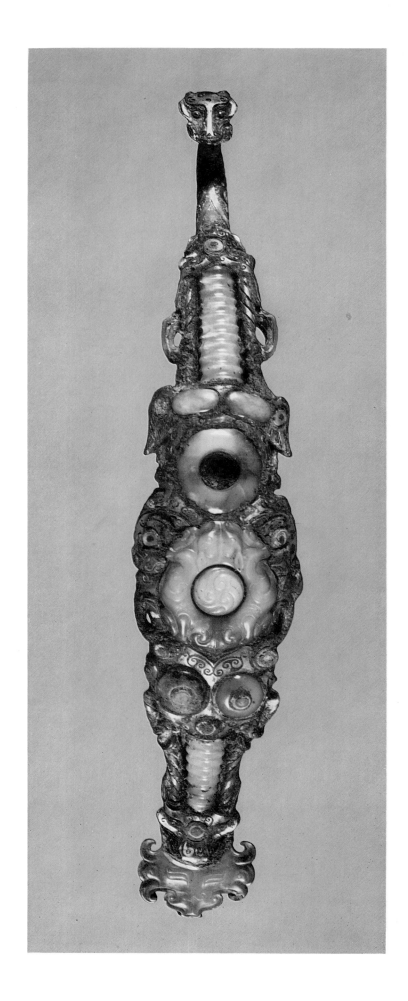

32

帯鉤　　　周時代

BELT HOOK　　CHOU DYNASTY

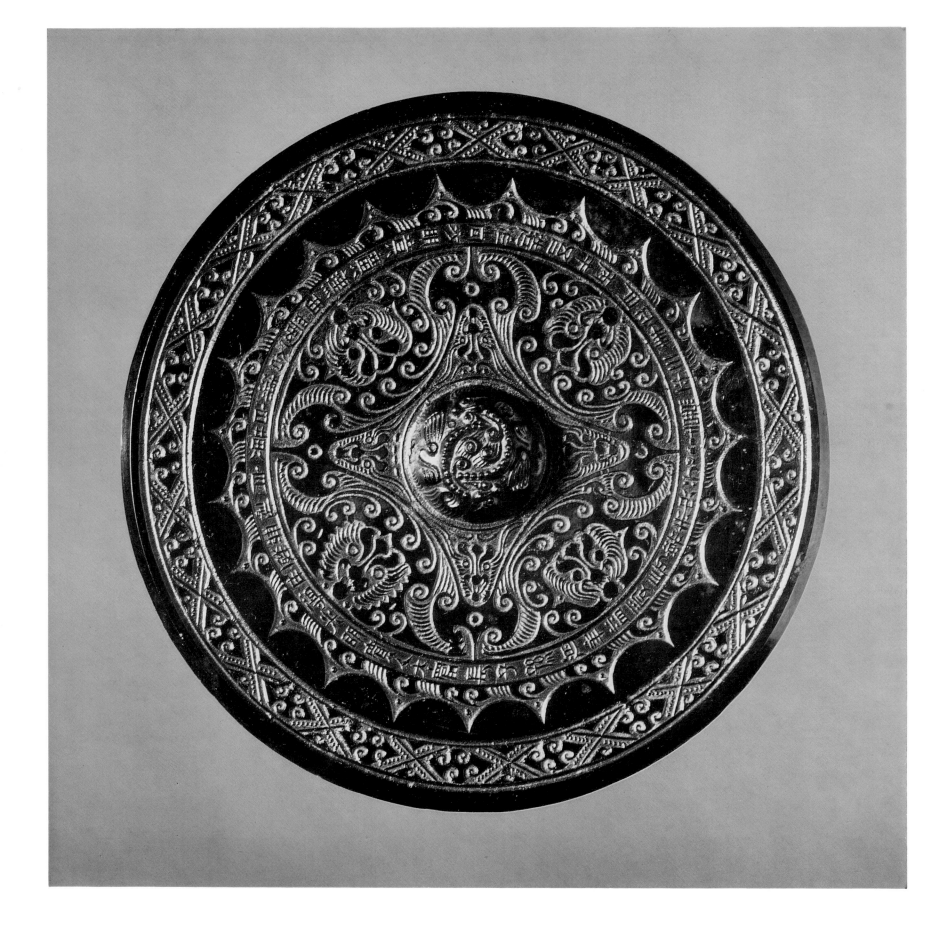

33
青銅鏡　　　漢時代
BRONZE MIRROR　　HAN DYNASTY

II

絵画
PAINTING

34
水月観音図
KUAN-YIN OF THE WATER MOON
宋時代
SUNG DYNASTY

35
洛神図（部分）　　　　　宋時代
NYMPH OF THE LO RIVER (DETAIL)　　　SUNG DYNASTY

36 • 37
内人雙六図 （部分）　　宋時代
LADIES PLAYING DOUBLE SIXES (DETAIL)　　SUNG DYNASTY

38
郭熙　　渓山秋霽図（部分）　　　　　　　　　　　宋時代
KUO HSI　　CLEARING AUTUMN SKIES OVER MOUNTAINS AND VALLEYS（DETAIL）　　SUNG DYNASTY

39
閻次于 山村帰騎図 宋時代
YEN TZ'U-YÜ HOSTELRY IN THE MOUNTAINS SUNG DYNASTY

40

毛益　　柳燕図　　　　　　　　　　　　　宋時代
MAO I　　SWALLOWS AND WILLOW TREE　　SUNG DYNASTY

41

林庭桂　　　五百羅漢図
LIN T'ING-KUEI　　LOHANS LAUNDERING
宋時代
SUNG DYNASTY

禮部侍郎致仕王渙九十歲

42
王渙像　　　　　　　　　宋時代
PORTRAIT OF WANG HUAN　　SUNG DYNASTY

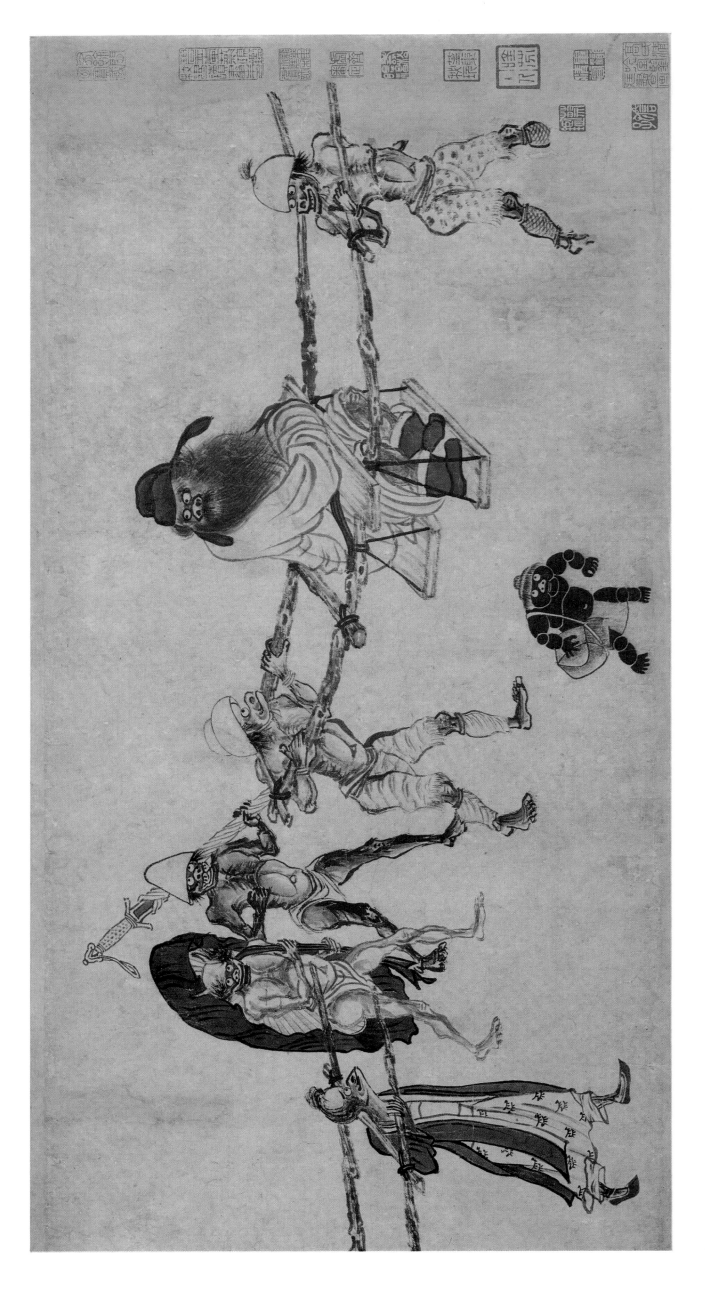

43

龔開　中山出遊図（部分）　　宋時代
KUNG K'AI　CHUNG K'UEI THE DEMON-QUELLER (DETAIL)　　SUNG DYNASTY

44
李山　風雪杉松図（部分）　金時代
LI SHAN　WIND AND SNOW IN THE FIR-PINES (DETAIL)　CHIN DYNASTY

45
鄒復雷　　　春消息図（部分）　　　元時代
TSOU FU-LEI　　A BREATH OF SPRING (DETAIL)　　YÜAN DYNASTY

一氣為春玄必圓誰
物消息付寒梅蕊珠
仙妬如夷巧偷先蒼玄
風特地來
用圉河元韻如題

46

錢選　　　来禽梔子図（部分）　　　元時代
CH'IEN HSÜAN　　　CRABAPPLE AND GARDENIA (DETAIL)　　　YÜAN DYNASTY

趙孟頫　　二羊図　　元時代
CHAO MENG-FU　　SHEEP AND GOAT　　YÜAN DYNASTY

己酉歳宋仲温為
長卿寓万竹窗

48
宋克　　万竹図（部分）　　元時代
SUNG K'O　　MYRIAD BAMBOO (DETAIL)　　YÜAN DYNASTY

49

戴進　　漁楽図（部分）　　明時代

TAI CHIN　　FISHERMAN ON THE RIVER (DETAIL)　　MING DYNASTY

50　唐寅　南遊図（部分）　明時代
TANG YIN　JOURNEY TO THE SOUTH (DETAIL)　MING DYNASTY

51
鎖諫図 （部分）　　　　　　　　明時代
CH'EN YÜAN-TA ADMONISHING LIU TS'UNG (DETAIL)　　MING DYNASTY

52
湖上陰屋図　　　　　明時代
BOAT MOORED BY A STORMY LAKE　　MING DYNASTY

53

王世昌　　　　松陰書屋図　　　　　　　明時代

WANG SHIH-CH'ANG　　SCHOLAR'S ABODE IN THE MOUNTAINS　　MING DYNASTY

54

仇英　　　倣李唐山水図（部分）　　　　　　　　明時代

55

王時敏　　　倣巨然山水図　　　清時代
WANG SHIH-MIN　　LANDSCAPE IN THE STYLE OF CHÜ-JAN　　CH'ING DYNASTY

56
石濤　　桃源図（部分）　　　清時代
TAO-CHI　　PEACH BLOSSOM SPRING (DETAIL)　　CH'ING DYNASTY

57

王翬　　富春山居図（部分）　　　　　　　　清時代

WANG HUI　　DWELLING IN THE FU-CH'UN MOUNTAINS (DETAIL)　　CH'ING DYNASTY

董巨風韻元季四家中大癡得之
最深多開生面明季三百年來
董宗伯僕骨天成入其堂奧在
錢正傳先奉半一人而已余切慕
家訓早歲目染著有一知半解未
能自以為是也
惟恨先生同立
暢春內乾情好多同官春隈余寫
澄園園長岑余微山樵之志植本畫
光影擬詩色于久一幅七佳群假南
薛寫以贈之并
正
原祁丙戌子春畫并題
王原祁

58
王原祁　　倣黄公望山水図　　清時代
WANG YÜAN-CH'I　　LANDSCAPE IN THE STYLE OF HUANG KUNG-WANG　　CH'ING DYNASTY

59
山水図　　　　　　　　　　　　　　金時代
MOUNTAIN AND RIVER LANDSCAPE　　CHIN DYNASTY

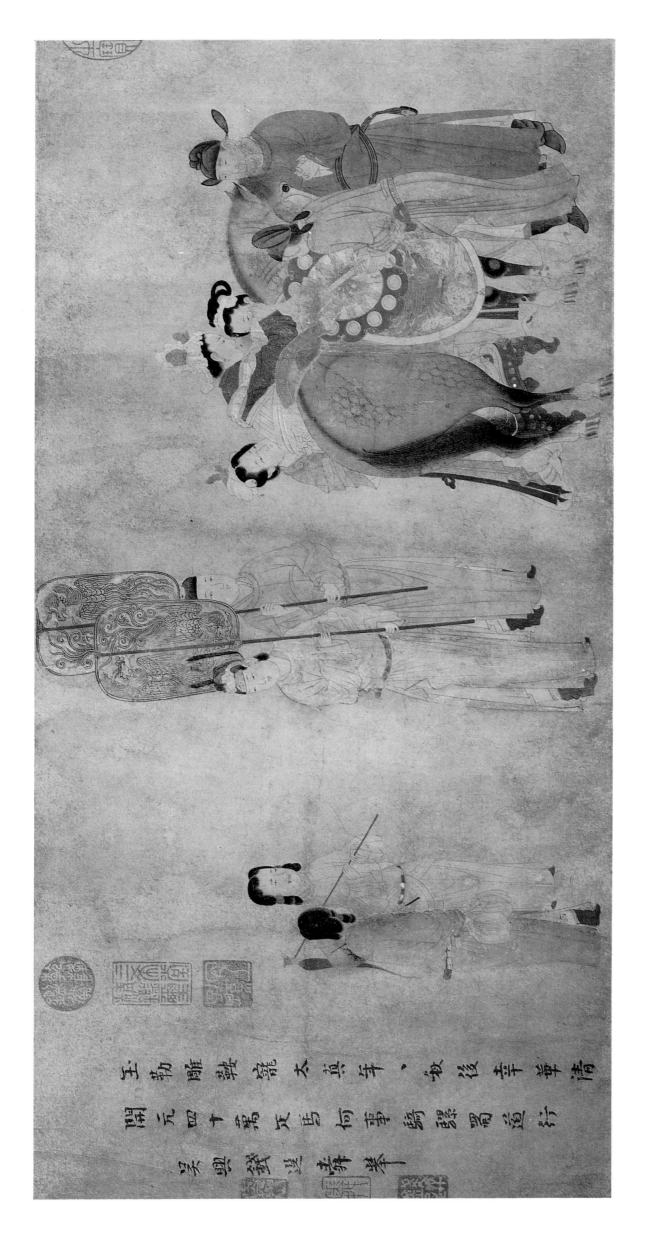

60　　錢選　　楊貴妃上馬圖（部分）　　元時代

CH'IEN HSÜAN　　YANG KUEI-FEI MOUNTING A HORSE (DETAIL)　　YÜAN DYNASTY

61

趙雍　　臨李公麟人馬圖　　元時代
CHAO YUNG　HORSE AND GROOM　YÜAN DYNASTY

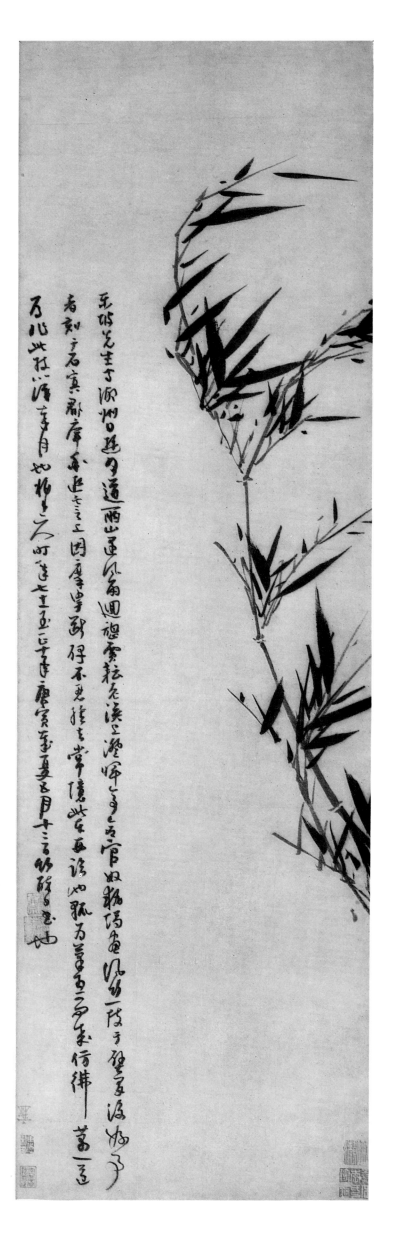

呉鎮　　墨竹図　　元時代
WU CHEN　　BAMBOO IN THE WIND　　YÜAN DYNASTY

63
王蒙　　　夏山隠居図　　　　　　　　　　　　　　　　　元時代
WANG MENG　　SECLUDED DWELLINGS IN THE SUMMER MOUNTAINS　　YÜAN DYNASTY

64
提婆王（部分）　元時代
DEVA KING (DETAIL)　YÜAN DYNASTY

65

夏景　　　岳陽楼図　　　　　元時代
HSIA YUNG　　THE YÜEH-YANG TOWER　　YÜAN DYNASTY

劉玨　臨安山色図（部分）　明時代
LIU CHÜEH　MOUNTAIN SCENERY ON THE WAY TO LIN-AN (DETAIL)　MING DYNASTY

文徴明　　　赤壁勝遊図（部分）　　明時代
WEN CHENG-MING　　THE RED CLIFF (DETAIL)　　MING DYNASTY

68
陸治　　潯陽秋色図（部分）　　　明時代
LU CHIH　　AUTUMN COLORS AT HSÜN-YANG (DETAIL)　　MING DYNASTY

道人懶筆看毛物
偶施小黃作姥遊人
言杏晨可摘賣桂禰
街頸試買不

徐渭　　　　杏花図（部分）　　　　　明時代
HSÜ WEI　　APRICOT BLOSSOMS (DETAIL)　　MING DYNASTY

70

陳洪綬　　　　　山水人物図　　　　　明時代
CH'EN HUNG-SHOU　　LANDSCAPE WITH FIGURE　　MING DYNASTY

71

龔賢　　山水画冊　　清時代
KUNG HSIEN　WINTER LANDSCAPE　CH'ING DYNASTY

玉女窻中有人同夢、在水邊林下似余五年前為華亭沈君沃田畫
梅花帳子題句也時沈君方納姬金屋有詩紀事用儔多艷稱之本余又用
胭脂螺黛畫山小幅復書前詞家有明珠十斛之人者贈之何如
己卯嘉平月三日奉寄
鶴亭先生上鄉大雅之賞七十三翁杭郡金農記

72
金農　　梅花図　　清時代
CHIN NUNG　　PLUM BLOSSOMS　　CH'ING DYNASTY

III

彫刻・陶磁・漆工
SCULPTURE, CERAMICS AND LACQUER

73
仏坐像　　　　六朝時代
SEATED BUDDHA　　SIX DYNASTIES

74
石灰石の菩薩像（部分）　　　　北魏時代
GRAY LIMESTONE BODHISATTVA (DETAIL)　　NORTHERN WEI DYNASTY

75

白大理石の樹下菩薩半跏思惟像　　　　　北斉時代

WHITE MARBLE BODHISATTVA SEATED IN MEDITATION　　　NORTHERN CH'I DYNASTY

76
灰色の石灰石の棺台（部分）　　　北斉時代
GRAY LIMESTONE FUNERARY COUCH (DETAIL)　　　NORTHERN CH'I DYNASTY

77

灰色の石灰石の邪鬼　　　北斉時代
GRAY LIMESTONE DEMON FIGURE　　NORTHERN CH'I DYNASTY

78

石灰石の浅浮彫阿弥陀浄土図（部分）　　　北斉時代

LIMESTONE BAS-RELIEF, AMITABHA PARADISE (DETAIL)　　　NORTHERN CH'I DYNASTY

79
仏像　隋時代
BUDDHA　SUI DYNASTY

80
菩薩　　　唐時代
BODHISATTVA　T'ANG DYNASTY

81
菩薩　　唐時代
BODHISATTVA　T'ANG DYNASTY

82

十一面観音　　　　　　　　　　　　　　　　　　　　　　　　　　　唐時代
ELEVEN-HEADED KUAN-YIN, EKADASĀMUKHA-AVALOKITESVARA　　　T'ANG DYNASTY

83
仏坐像　　宋時代
SEATED BUDDHA　SUNG DYNASTY

84
菩薩坐像　　　　元時代
SEATED BODHISATTVA　YÜAN DYNASTY

85
白陶の壺　　　　　殷時代
WHITE EARTHENWARE JAR　　　SHANG DYNASTY

86
黒釉の越窯の水指　　　　　六朝時代
BLACK-GLAZED YÜEH WARE EWER　　SIX DYNASTIES

87
白磁の水指　　　唐時代
WHITE PORCELAIN EWER　　T'ANG DYNASTY

88
土器質の瓶　　唐時代
EARTHENWARE JAR　　T'ANG DYNASTY

89
竜泉窯の花生け　宋時代
LUNG-CH'ÜAN VASE　SUNG DYNASTY

90
北方青磁の瓶　　宋時代
NORTHERN CELADON VASE　SUNG DYNASTY

91
均窯の瓶 　　　元時代
CHÜN WARE VASE 　　YÜAN DYNASTY

92
定窯の盌　　宋時代
TING WARE BOWL　SUNG DYNASTY

93
定窯の瓶　　　宋時代
TING WARE VASE　　SUNG DYNASTY

94
建窯の茶碗　　宋時代
CHIEN WARE BOWL　　SUNG DYNASTY

95
磁州窯の瓶　　宋時代
TZ'U-CHOU WARE VASE　SUNG DYNASTY

96
磁州窯の瓶　　　宋時代
TZ'U-CHOU WARE VASE　　SUNG DYNASTY

97
染付の酒保　　　明時代初め
BLUE-AND-WHITE CANTEEN　　EARLY MING DYNASTY

染付の皿　　　　明時代初め
BLUE-AND-WHITE DISH　　EARLY MING DYNASTY

99
染付の鉢　　　　明時代
BLUE-AND-WHITE BOWL　　MING DYNASTY

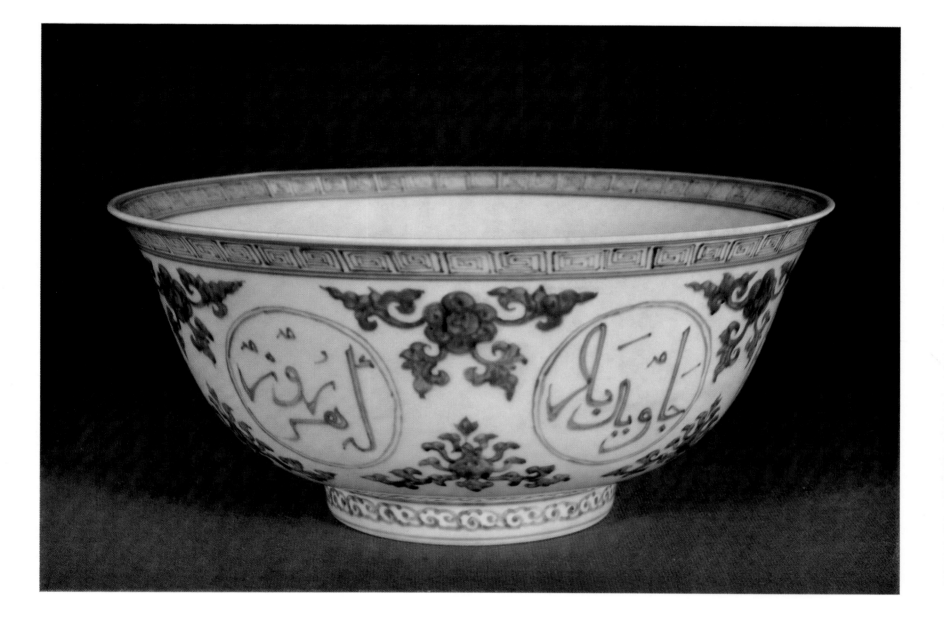

染付の鉢　　　　　　明時代
BLUE-AND-WHITE BOWL　　MING DYNASTY

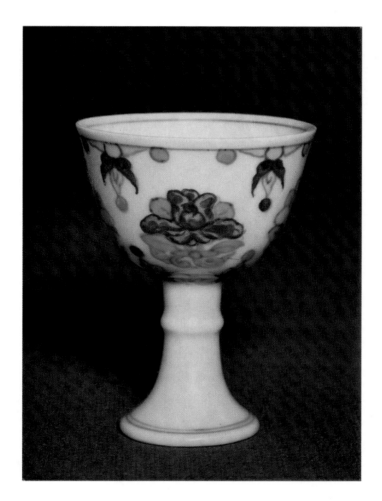

101
闘彩の高足杯　　明時代
TOU-TS'AI STEM-CUP　　MING DYNASTY

102
古月軒の瓶　　　　　清時代
KU-YÜEH-HSÜAN VASE　　CH'ING DYNASTY

103
古月軒の碗　　　　　清時代
KU-YÜEH-HSÜAN BOWL　　CH'ING DYNASTY

104
銀製鉢　　唐時代
SILVER BOWL　　T'ANG DYNASTY

105
銀製杯　　唐時代
SILVER CUP　　T'ANG DYNASTY

106		107		108	
金製天女	唐時代	銀製合子	唐時代	金製蓋付小壺	明時代
GOLD APSARAS	T'ANG DYNASTY	SILVER COVERED BOX	T'ANG DYNASTY	GOLD COVERED JAR	MING DYNASTY

109
トルコ石添装金製如意　　清時代
GOLD AND TURQUOISE JU-I　　CH'ING DYNASTY

110
香炉　　明時代
INCENSE BURNER　MING DYNASTY

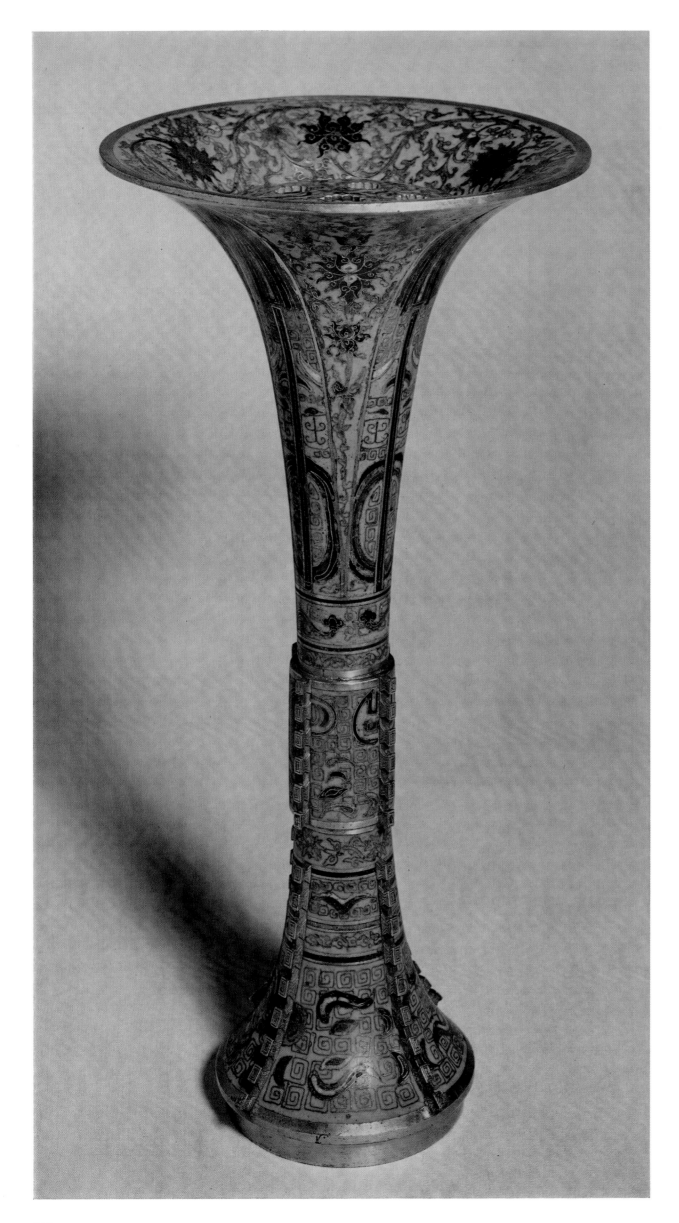

111
花器　清時代
VASE　CH ING DYNASTY

112
高脚杯　　周時代
STEM CUP　　CHOU DYNASTY

136
鉢　周時代
BOWL　CHOU DYNASTY

114
漆鉢　　　　　　宋時代
LACQUER BOWL　　SUNG DYNASTY

115
彫漆合子　　明時代
COVERED BOX　　MING DYNASTY

116
仏立像　　　　　北魏時代
STANDING BUDDHA　　NORTHERN WEI DYNASTY

117
碑像　北魏時代
STELE　NORTHERN WEI DYNASTY

118
三尊仏　　　　隋時代
BUDDHAIST TRINITY　　SUI DYNASTY

119

神将像頭部　　　　　唐時代

HEAD OF A GUARDIAN FIGURE　　T'ANG DYNASTY

120
荷葉文盤　　唐時代
DISH　　　T'ANG DYNASTY

121
舞人俑　　　　　　唐時代
BURIAL FIGURINE OF DANCER　　T'ANG DYNASTY

122

唾壺　唐時代
VASE　T'ANG DYNASTY

123
合子　　　　北宋時代
COVERED CONTAINER　　NORTHERN SUNG DYNASTY

124
双耳壺　北宋時代
JAR　　NORTHERN SUNG DYNASTY

125
壺　宋時代
VASE　SUNG DYNASTY

126
花生け 南宋時代
VASE SOUTHERN SUNG DYNASTY

127
蓋付容器　　　　明時代
STEM BOWL WITH COVER　　MING DYNASTY

128
壺　明時代
JAR　MING DYNASTY

129
花生け　清時代
VASE　CH'ING DYNASTY

130
花生け　清時代
VASE　　CH'ING DYNASTY

131
彫漆合子　　　　明時代
COVERED LACQUER BOX　　MING DYNASTY

Explanation of Plates

1 *KU*   51.18

Inscription of one character
Height, 33.0 cm. (13 in.); width, 19.0 cm. (7 1/2 in.)
Shang dynasty, middle-late Anyang, 12th–11th century B.C.

This is the largest and perhaps finest of the three *ku* in the collection. Most striking are the bold segmented flanges that rise from the bottom of the vessel to the top, with three interruptions, and protrude beyond the edge of the lip. Each flange is composed of four segments, corresponding to the four horizontal zones of the design. The effect of this segmentation is to further emphasize the quadripartite division of the decor which imposes "corners" and "sides" of a square or rectangular vessel on one actually round in section and make the piece as a whole conform better to the late Shang taste for the architectonic and severe. The casting is exceptionally deep and fine all over, and the surface is covered with a uniform gray-green patina.

2 *HU*   49.5

Height, 17.5 cm. (6 7/8 in.); width, 11.7 cm. (4 5/8 in.)
Shang dynasty; middle Anyang, 12th century B.C.

The combination of purely abstract surface pattern with motifs of minimal zoomorphic nature is most often associated with shapes that seem derived from ceramic vessels, and such a derivation is suggested in this small covered *hu*. The designs on the neck and lid, lacking any separation between the motifs proper and the usual ground of spiral fillings, are of a variety known from some of the earlier vessels of the Anyang period, and presumably originated in a carving or engraving technique. The patina is a smooth, even gray-green on the raised surfaces, and the casting is extremely fine.

3 *KUANG*   38.5

Height, 23.5 cm. (9 1/4 in.); width, 31.1 cm. (12 1/4 in.)
Shang dynasty, middle Anyang, 12th century B.C.

This unique *kuang*, while it conveys an effect of free fantasy in its metamorphic animal components, is simpler in design than it appears at first sight. Seen from the front, the lid terminates in a boldly conceived feline head, while the back end shows the face of a great horned owl looking upwards. The body of the vessel takes the general form of seated fowl with a curious blunt-nosed head with ears. Fine casting in low relief covers the entire surface with *lei-wen*, various dragon types, and with scale-like feathers on the neck, breast and lower side of the fowl. The stylized wings on the sides and the legs and claws on the foot of the vessel are in higher relief and more boldly designed. Smooth, sage-green patina covers the entire surface.

4 *HUO*   42.1

Height, 18.5 cm. (7 1/4 in.); width, 21.0 cm. (8 1/4 in.)
Shang dynasty, middle Anyang, 12th century B.C.

The squat, heavy-set vessel and lid take on an anthropomorphic character with the human face on top and the bent arms at the sides. The creature has a serpentine body beginning behind the head and making one complete spiral turn around the vessel; concentric rectangles bordered by a scale band above and a different band below cover the body. A ground of *lei-wen* covers the rest of the vessel. The surface is covered with a smooth,

gray-green patina with small areas of malachite encrustation. So far this vessel is unique among extant Chinese bronzes. Although called a *huo* by way of classification, it actually has little in common with other pouring vessels of the Shang period.

5 *HUO*   36.6

Height, 17.5 cm. (6 7/8 in.); width, 21.3 cm. (8 3/8 in.)
Shang dynasty, late Anyang, 11th century B.C.

The vessel takes the shape of an elephant executed in the round. On the lid is the same elephant repeated in miniature. Among early Chinese bronze vessels in elephant form, this *huo* is relatively naturalistic. It may be that the bronze artisan was simply allowed more freedom in natural forms, unrestrained by the dictates of conventional vessel shapes, and used his freedom to practice greater individuality. The realism is limited to the shape of the piece, however, since the surface ornament belongs to the standard Shang repertory.

6 *YU*   42.14

Height, 24.2 cm. (9 1/2 in.); width, 21.5 cm. (8 1/2 in.)
Shang dynasty, middle-late Anyang, 12th–11th century B.C.

The double-owl *yu* is common among Shang and early Chou vessels. Among the numerous examples known, those with bodies bare of ornamentation make up the majority. The other group, to which this example belongs, are by contrast richly ornamented over their entire surfaces with symmetrically arranged animals on each side of the median line set against the customary spiral filling. On the wing and breast areas scale patterns, both plain and with *lei-wen*, are used to simulate feathers. The birds on the upper part of the vessel are in high relief and seem to have been made separately from identical molds or stamps. The raised circles in the narrow band around the rim appear to be from impressions made in the mould sections by the end of a tube. The surface of the *yu* is covered with an elegant tin-oxide patina tinged uniformly pale green.

7 *KUANG*   61.33

Height, 31.4 cm. (12 3/8 in.); width, 31.3 cm. (12 3/8 in.)
Early Chou dynasty, late 11th–early 10th century B.C.

The most striking feature of this exceptionally powerful vessel is the great monster mask at the front of the lid with its curling horns, like the horns of the *Ovis poli*. The back of the lid is again a bird mask with something like buffalo horns at the top. A fish, a tiger, and an elephant are among the animals identifiable on the *lei-wen* ground. The body consists of a bird-like design at the front with a beak protruding below the spout. Ears project at right angles from the vessel behind the bold round eyes, and the wings consist of coiled dragons.

The relatively naturalistic rendering of animals, the free and unsymmetrical combination of animal forms into crowded, sometimes teeming compositions, and the use of striation on animal bodies, are characteristic of Ordos and other nomadic bronze art in later centuries, suggesting that this style was somehow affiliated with, or influenced by, the styles of some nomadic people of the borderlands of China.

8 *KUEI*   31.10

Height, 23.5 cm. (9 1/4 in.); width, 36.5 cm. (14 3/8 in.)
Early Chou dynasty, late 11th–early 10th century B.C.

The vessel has four heavy handles, and the surface is dominated by two bands of long spikes, each arranged in groups of twelve between the handles and the intermediate segmented flanges.

The apparently short-lived early Chou style was characterized by a profusion of heavy angular projections that violate the surface outline of the vessels, and by a reduction in the repertory of animal motifs so that a single animal, here a horned bovine, dominates the iconographic theme. The band of vertical ribbing is another feature confined to bronzes of the early Chou period. The spikes that protrude from the bands above and below this represent a last extreme stage of a development that began in the Shang dynasty with an allover diaper pattern featuring low bosses in the center of each lozenge.

9 *FANG-I*   30.54

Inscription of 187 characters in the lid and 188 in the bottom.
Height, 35.6 cm. (14 in.); width, 24.7 cm. (9 3/4 in.)
Early Chou dynasty, late 11th–early 10th century B.C.

The *fang-i*, part of the Nieh-ling set, reportedly was found at Lo-yang. All features of the decor bear out the early Chou date indicated by the long inscription. The motif occupying the band just below the lid, a beast's head with the split body of a serpent extending to each side, is seen on other vessels datable to the early Chou period. The birds in the lowest band are also typical of the period, although not unknown earlier. The pierced hooked flanges, in particular, carry to a further point the late Shang tendency toward disrupting the outline of the vessel with multiple projections and so violating the self-enclosed quality of vessels of the 'classic' Anyang phase.

10 TIGER   35.21

Length, 75.2 cm. (29 5/8 in.); height, 25.2 cm. (9 7/8 in.)
Chou dynasty, 9th century B.C.

The tiger's gaping jaws and curled talons lend an intense ferocity to its appearance. Broad, raised ornamental bands, closely related to designs found on ritual bronzes dating from the same period, cover the body suggesting the actual striping of a tiger's coat. Equally indicative of the artist's close observation of nature is the subtle undulating contour of the back. Seen in silhouette, the contour swells over the shoulders and haunches, dipping in the center and, finally, culminating in a taut curl at the end of the tail.

A rectangular opening on the back of the tiger suggests that the animal may have been used as a structural support. The tiger, one of a pair, is said to have been found in Pao-chi Hsien, Shensi province.

11 JUGGLER   51.7

Height, 16.4 cm. (6 1/2 in.); width, 05.3 cm. (2 1/8 in.)
Chou dynasty, 6th–5th century B.C.

The juggler stands with his right knee bent, left arm raised and head turned to one side. The right arm supports a pole atop which a bear is balancing. The summary modeling of the figure, somewhat relieved by incised linear decoration and the slightly more plastic handling of the sword fastened with a belt at the back, contrasts with the sensitive articulation of the small bear curled precariously at the top of the pole. The vivid animation of the bear reflects the Chinese concern for animal sculpture from earliest times, while the ungainly stance of the juggler betrays a still undeveloped ability in depicting the human figure.

12 *PIEN-HU*   15.103

Height, 31.2 cm. (12 1/4 in.); width, 30.5 cm. (12 in.)
Late Chou dynasty, late 4th–early 3rd century B.C.

This type of vessel, known as a *pien-hu* or flat *hu*, does not make its appearance until near the end of the Chou period—probably not before 400 B.C. There are animal mask escutcheons with pendant loose rings on two sides. The whole surface is elaborately decorated with a broad, bold geometric pattern, the flat areas of which are broken up by an arrangement of extremely fine spirals, hooks and volutes. This pattern appears to have been executed by cutting out the surface of the bronze and inlaying it with silver. The bronze is evenly covered with a dark brown patina showing some areas of malachite and cuprite incrustation.

13 TERMINAL ORNAMENT   32.14

Length, 25.5 cm. (10 1/6 in.)
Chou dynasty, 5th–3rd century B.C.

The terminal ornament modelled in the form of a dragon head has a square hole at the top, probably to hold a cotter pin for attachment to another member, perhaps to the end of a chariot pole. The bronze is overlaid with gold and engraved with curvilinear designs that are somewhat obscured by patination. The teeth and eyeballs are overlaid with silver, while the pupils of the eyes are of glass. A small loop under the lower jaw may have served for the suspension of a tassel. The terminal ornament is said to have been excavated in one of the horse pits near the entrance of a tomb at Chin-ts'un in Honan province.

14 INCENSE BURNER, *PO-SHAN HSIANG-LU*   47.15

Height, 17.9 cm. (7 1/16 in.); width, 10.0 cm. (3 15/16 in.)
Late Chou–Early Han dynasty, 5th–3rd century B.C.

The conical cover of the incense burner takes the form of twelve mountain peaks surrounding a thirteenth central peak. The tops of nine of these peaks in the three lower levels are modelled in the round, with a vent for the release of incense vapor concealed behind. In the center of each of the three peaks are low relief castings depicting human figures and animals. The inlaid silver hatching indicating fur on the animals is typical of the Huai style. The rim of the cover, as well as the surface and stem of the bowl, are decorated with silver and gold inlay patterns with turquoise and carnelian insets. Three coiled dragons are cast in relief on the base.

15 JADE BATTLE-AXE *PI* DISC   68.48

Diameter, 22.5 cm. (8 1/8 in.)
Shang dynasty
Gift of Mr. and Mrs. Eugene Meyer

The composite shape of this type of ritual jade is derived from the *pi* disc and *ch'i* battle-axe. Pairs of six-toothed flanges on either side of the disc are neatly beveled from the flat surface. The lower flaring edge also is beveled. The overall shape of the disc, as well as the refined carving of such purely aesthetic details as the flanges, are eloquent reminders of sophisticated Shang dynasty taste.

16 BRONZE AND JADE *KO*   41.5

Length, 41.9 cm. (16 1/2 in.)
Shang dynasty

The *ko*, or dagger-axe, is the most common type of ancient Chinese weapon now known. Ceremonial replicas of the more sturdy bronze prototypes occasionally were made with turquoise-inlaid bronze handles and jade blades. In this example, the *t'ao-t'ieh* and *k'uei* designs are made with turquoise tesserae inset into frets which were cast with the handle. The perforated tang or shafting plate (*nei*) is heavily patinated with cuprite and malachite. This *ko*, which is similar to several examples found at Anyang in Honan province, also may have been excavated at that site.

17 JADE CEREMONIAL BLADE, *HU*   68.38
Width, 07.0 cm. (2 3/4 in.); length, 19.0 cm. (7 1/2 in.)
Chou dynasty, 5th–3rd century B.C.
Gift of Mr. and Mrs. Eugene Meyer

Ceremonial jade versions of utilitarian stone or metal artifacts often were embellished with extraordinarily delicate ornamentation. A wide notched border surrounds three sides of this ceremonial blade of *hu* type. Six perforations on the blade proper are connected by straight engraved lines. The principal motifs on the border are horned dragons in raised bands of varying width.

18 JADE PLAQUE   32.43
Width, 06.1 cm. (2 7/16 in.); length, 14.8 cm. (5 13/16 in.)
Chou dynasty, 5th–3rd century B.C.

The precise technical skill and keen sense of design characteristic of jade carvings made during the late Chou dynasty are evident in this tiger plaque. Parts of the body are ornamented with a variety of abstract designs or stylized bird and floral forms. Narrow bands enclose and articulate the animal's body. The plaque, one of a pair in the collection, is said to have been excavated at Lo-yang in Honan province.

19 JADE NECKLACE   30.27
Length, 40.7 cm. (16 1/16 in.)
Chou dynasty, 5th–3rd century B.C.

Groups of jade carving found together as a composite ornament are quite unusual. These ten pieces of jade are attached to four strands of braided gold wire. A pair of female dancers form the upper section of the pendant, while an oval double-tiger pendant is flanked by single-tiger spirals in the lower section. Conical and cylindrical beads complete the necklace. The jade pieces are carved in relief and incised on both sides. The necklace was excavated at Chin-ts'un in Honan province.

20 JADE COVERED CUP   47.10
Overall height, 12.1 cm. (4 3/4 in.)
Chou dynasty, 5th–3rd century B.C.

Feline animals silhouetted against a background of small spirals ornament the body of the cup. Incised linear bands enclosing the main body of the cup repeat elements found on the felines. These elements, suggestive of both animal forms and pure ornament, are indicative of a late Chou date. The three short legs are ornamented by stylized masks. A similar mask in low relief is carved behind the handle. Three winged felines adorn the cover.

21 BELT HOOK   49.25
Bronze with gold and turquoise; length, 19.7 cm. (7 3/4 in.)
Chou dynasty, 3rd century B.C.

The belt hook is decorated with an imbricated pattern of turquoise inlay in gold cloisons. Bolder gold band inlay designs suggest abstract bird-derived forms.

22 BELT HOOK   49.6
Bronze inlaid with gold and silver; length, 12.3 cm. (4 7/8 in.), width, 6.0 cm. (2 3/8 in.)
Chou dynasty, ca. 300–250 B.C.

The interlaced dragon design, inlaid in gold on a background of silver dots, is a sophisticated adaptation of a motif found on ritual bronzes dating as early as the 6th–5th century B.C. Abstract

curvilinear wings are a later innovation. The spade-shaped belt hook is unusually large and heavy.

23 BELT HOOK   54.120
Jade with gold mounting; length, 12.3 cm. (4 13/16 in.), width, 2.5 cm. (1 in.)
Chou dynasty, 5th–3rd century B.C.

The combination of white jade and gold results in an unusually sumptuous belt hook. Two birds at the middle of the belt hook, on the section which holds the large button, form a transition between the paired gold-capped jade tubes and the single piece of jade connecting with the animal-headed terminal hook. Both the modelling of gold and jade carving exhibit the extremely fine workmanship which is characteristic of so many late Chou dynasty artifacts. The belt hook is said to have been excavated at Shou Hsien in Anhui province.

24 BELT HOOK   49.24
Bronze covered with gold sheet; length, 10.3 cm. (4 1/16 in.)
Chou dynasty, 3rd century B.C.

Both the front and back surfaces of the belt hook are covered with cloud patterns and circles. The head of the hook is animal-shaped, with inlaid striated lines to indicate the eyes.

25 BRONZE MIRROR   36.3
Diameter, 19.5 cm. (7 11/14 in.)
Chou dynasty, 5th–3rd century B.C.

The reverse of the mirror is a single flat surface with neither knob-seat nor rim raised above it. Six fantastic beasts are symmetrically intertwined in the main field of decoration. A gold and silver pattern of volutes and triangles, so characteristic of Late Eastern Chou period, is inlaid in the outer band. The designs are closely related to those found on objects excavated at Chin-ts'un in Honan province.

26 BRONZE MIRROR   44.8
Height, 15.9 cm. (6 1/4 in.); width, 15.9 cm. (6 1/4 in.)
T'ang dynasty

Floral designs, which appear to have become popular in China with the introduction of Buddhism, were particularly common during the T'ang dynasty. The central boss of this mirror is decorated with a cut gold and silver pattern inlaid onto a brown lacquer background. Another inlaid floral design surrounds the boss. Four silver phoenixes are placed one in each corner of the mirror, separated by small gold branches, birds and butterflies.

27 BRONZE MIRROR   30.45
Diameter, 22.0 cm. (8 11/16 in.)
T'ang dynasty

During the T'ang dynasty, Chinese metal craftsmen introduced floral-shaped mirrors. In this example, the outline of the mirror is similar to an eight-petalled lotus blossom. The face of the bronze mirror is silvery in color, but heavily encrusted with a green patina. Inset on the back of the mirror is a thin sheet of gold depicting floral scrolls and birds enframed by curling tendrils. The designs are in repoussé, a technique whereby ornamentation is made by hammering or pressing on the reverse side of the metal. These designs and background of small punched circles have close parallels in silver mirrors of the period.

28 *HU*   57.22
Height, 44.8 cm. (17 5/8 in.); width, 26.6 cm. (10 1/2 in.)
Late Chou dynasty, 5th century B.C.

The tall graceful round vessel has two animal handles in the shape of stylized tigers with heads turned backward and tongues protruded. The animals are richly decorated in intaglio and the dark patina set off by copper inserted in the fossae. There are four main decorative registers all consisting of interlocking dragon forms executed in broad bands covered with volutes and spirals in intaglio. These registers are separated by five braided rope patterns in relief. Similar decoration is arranged in ogival panels extending above the top-most rope pattern and hanging below the lower one; related decorations surround the foot. The vessel is finely cast and covered with a uniform dark brownish patina interrupted only occasionally by malachite encrustation on one side. The extraordinary fineness and precision of decor, combined with the unusually good state of preservation, make it one of the outstanding monuments of this style.

29 *CHIEN*   39.5

Inscription of six characters on the inside
Height, 22.8 cm. (9 in.); width, 51.7 cm. (20 3/8 in.)
Late Chou dynasty, 5th century B.C.

The large basin has four handles topped by monster masks, while loose flattened rings with intaglio decoration depend from two of them. The surface is divided into three principal bands, each decorated with highly stylized interlocking dragon forms depicted in broad bands covered with fine spirals and triangles in intaglio. The principal decorative zones are separated by braided rope bands in relief, and a third such band surrounds the foot. Around the outer edge of the lip is a band of cowries. The surface is covered with an even, pale green patina with a moderate amount of granular encrustation.

Since the inscription refers to the Chih family of the state of Chin, which was extinguished in 453 B.C., the vessel must have been made prior to that date.

30 *TOU*   39.41

Height, 15.5 cm. (6 1/8 in.); width, 18.7 cm. (7 3/8 in.)
Late Chou dynasty, 4th century B.C.

The gold-inlaid design on the *tou* is of special importance. It is clearly derived from the intertwined animal patterns that dominate bronze relief decor of the sixth and fifth centuries. The gold design is a translation of these animal patterns into a new medium, with the main configurations preserved but the elaborate fillings and other ornaments eliminated in a drastic simplification imposed in part, no doubt, by the limitations of the inlay technique.

31 *LIEN*   51.5

Height, 17.8 cm. (7 in.); width, 25.4 cm. (10 in.)
Han dynasty, 2nd–1st century B.C.

The cylindrical vessel is supported by three feet in the shape of crouching bears, while the surface is covered with two horizontal bands showing fabulous beasts and birds in a mountainous landscape. The design is in rather high relief, evidently cast in the rough and then finished with tooling, chiseling and incising of exceptional skill. The complexity and refinement of the ornamentation contrasts with other *lien* of this type. The animals and demons are in several registers, or levels, which appear to indicate, ambiguously, both height and distance. The overlapping of planes is elaborately and effectively managed, with animals emerging from behind hills at several points. The entire surface is covered with smooth, gray-green tin-oxide patina.

32 BELT HOOK   54.121

Bronze with gold, silver, jade and glass; length, 22.0 cm. (8 11/16 in.); width, 4.4 cm. (1 3/4 in.)
Chou dynasty, 5th–3rd century B.C.

An unusually elaborate piece, this belt hook is a composite of animal forms, ornamented with jade inlays and gilding. There is a design in silver on the back. The belt hook is said to have come from Ch'ang-sha in Hunan province. Similar round jade inlays as well as alternating gilded and non-gilded spirals are found on a large belt hook excavated at Hui-hsien, Honan province.

33 BRONZE MIRROR   39.38

Diameter, 18.2 cm. (7 3/16 in.)
Han dynasty, dated A.D. 174

Eight feline animal heads placed within the four points and outside the concave sides of the central square form the prominent decorative elements of this mirror. Boldly sweeping abstract lines with small spiral accents echo the curvilinear rhythms which define the animals' features and striped manes. The central knob is elaborately fashioned of two coiled winged creatures. A forty-seven character inscription cast in a band outside the main central design is dated in correspondence with A.D. 174. An even black patina covers the surface of the mirror.

34 KUAN-YIN OF THE WATER MOON   30.36

Ink and color on silk; height, 107.1 cm. (42 3/16 in.); width, 59.1 cm. (23 1/4 in.)
Sung dynasty

The Bodhisattva Kuan-yin is seated cross-legged on a lotus throne enframed by a flame-bordered nimbus. Attributes such as the flask and willow branch held in either hand, as well as the small seated figure of Amitabha in the Bodhisattva's headdress, clearly identify the deity. Smaller attendant Bodhisattvas flank the low altar placed before the lotus throne. In the lower register, four donor figures are depicted on either side of the central cartouche which contains an inscription dated in correspondence with 968. The bright mineral colors and hieratic composition are typical of Buddhist paintings of the period. The scroll is said to have come from Tun-huang in Kansu province.

35 NYMPH OF THE LO RIVER   14.53

Style of Ku K'ai-chih
Ink and color on silk; height, 24.0 cm. (9 7/16 in.); length, 310.0 cm. (122 1/16 in.)
Sung dynasty

The handscroll illustrates a poem written by Ts'ao Chih in A.D. 222, describing an encounter with the river goddess. Although traditionally attributed to Ku K'ai-chih, an artist who was active about A.D. 400, the painting probably is a faithful Sung dynasty copy. The figures, trees, clouds and mountains first were defined with even-width outlines and then filled in with color washes. While it is obvious that the stylized trees, clouds and mountains still are little more than stage props to set the scene for the activities of the figures, these tentative beginnings were of crucial importance in the development of Chinese landscape painting.

(The complete composition is reproduced on page 157.)

36. 37 LADIES PLAYING DOUBLE SIXES   39.37, 60.4

Style of Chou Fang
Ink and color on silk; height, 30.7 cm. (12 1/16 in.); length, 64.4 cm. (27 5/16 in.)
Sung dynasty, 10th–11th century

Chou Fang, who worked in the late eighth century, is noted for his paintings of plump, heavily coiffured palace ladies, based on the ample proportions of Yang Kuei-fei. In this Sung dynasty copy of a Chou Fang composition, two ladies are seated before a low table playing double-sixes, a game similar to backgammon. Two women stand to one side watching the game, while the figures of four servants carrying water and a basin, frame either side of the composition. The psychological awareness of the

figures is subtley revealed by their discreet gestures and glances. (The complete composition is reproduced on page 158.)

38 CLEARING AUTUMN SKIES OVER MOUNTAINS AND VALLEYS   16.538

Attributed to Kuo Hsi
Ink and light color on silk; height, 26.0 cm. (10 1/4 in.); length, 206.0 cm.
(81 3/8 in.)
Sung dynasty

Although Kuo Hsi is mentioned in records as one of the greatest landscape artists of the late 11th century, few genuine examples of his work are still extant. In this handscroll, the artist used moist ink washes to depict the towering, mist-shrouded mountain peaks. The foreground trees, buildings, and figures are rendered with more meticulous detail, as if seen emerging from obscuring mists. By contrasting foreground and background elements, the artist succeeded in creating an illusion of space and distance. The handscroll formerly was in the collection of the famous official and connoisseur, Tuan-fang (1861–1911).
(The complete composition is reproduced on page 159.)

39 HOSTELRY IN THE MOUNTAINS   35.10

by Yen Tz'u-yü
Ink and light color on silk; height, 25.3 cm. (10 in.); width, 25.8 cm.
(10 3/16 in.)
Sung dynasty

Yen Tz'u-yü, whose signature is written in small characters on a rock in the lower right, entered the Imperial Painting Academy around 1163. While never so famous as his brother, Yen Tz'u-p'ing, he was awarded the Golden Girdle, an emblem of high rank. The album leaf depicts a village situated on a rocky knoll by a river. A mounted traveller accompanied by a servant has just crossed the bridge on his way to the village. Formerly the album leaf was in the collection of Keng Chao-chung (1640–1686).
(Two leaves attributed to Chou Wen-chü that originally were part of the same album are reproduced on page 160.)

40 SWALLOWS AND WILLOW TREE   44.51

by Mao I (active 1165–1174)
Ink on silk; height 25.0 cm. (9 13/16 in.); width, 24.7 cm. (9 3/4 in.)
Sung dynasty

Mao I, who served in the Imperial Painting Academy during the late twelfth century, was a specialist in bird-and-flower paintings. His birds are said to have "looked as if about to fly

and sing." The sense of movement in this fan painting is extraordinarily vivid. The birds are depicted with minute dabs of ink, overlaid in various tones, without outlines. Their rumpled feathers, the bending of the willow branches and reeds below, as well as the waves on the water, indicate that there is a strong wind. The placement of a single swallow against a deep void at one side of the album leaf, is a typical compositional device of the Southern Sung period.

41 LOHANS LAUNDERING   02.224

by Lin T'ing-kuei
Ink and color on silk; height, 111.8 cm. (44 in.), width, 53.1 cm. (20 7/8 in.)
Sung dynasty

The painting of five lohans washing clothes, one of two scrolls in the collection, is part of a complete set depicting 500 lohans. The other scroll is signed by Chou Ch'i-ch'ang. The action takes place within the shallow recesses of a rocky embankment. Broad brushstrokes of ink define the contorted pines, rocks and rushing water, while the lohans and their servant are painted with precise outlines and opaque colors. An inscription in the lower right corner of the painting, written in gold and almost completely invisible, is dated in correspondence with 1178. Aside from these Buddhist paintings, Lin T'ing-kuei and Chou Ch'i-ch'ang are unknown in the history of Chinese painting.
(Another painting from the same set, this one painted by Chou Chi-ch'ang, is reproduced on page 160.)

42 PORTRAIT OF WANG HUAN   48.10

Ink and slight color on silk; height, 39.3 cm. (15 1/2 in.); width, 31.7 cm.
(12 3/8 in.)
Sung dynasty, 11th century

The portrait, from a set of five album leaves depicting the Five Old Men of Sui-yang, originally was mounted as a handscroll. Sui-yang is a district in Honan province where a shrine to the Five Old Men was once located. According to the inscriptions on the portraits, all of the men were eighty years old or more at the time. The portrait of Wang Huan evidently was done during his lifetime, or shortly after his death, and so dates from the eleventh century. The brief inscription identifies Wang Huan, gives his official title and states he was 90 years old at the time the portrait was painted. The portrait is formal and rather stiff, but the face is sensitively drawn. The drapery, slightly shaded, hangs naturally to suggest the form and stance of the body beneath.

(Another leaf from the same album, this one depicting Feng P'ing, is reproduced on page 161.)

43 CHUNG K'UEI THE DEMON-QUELLER   38.4
by Kung K'ai
Ink on paper; height, 32.8 cm. (12 15/16 in.), length, 169.5 cm. (56 3/4 in.)
Sung dynasty, 13th century

According to Kung K'ai's inscription, this handscroll depicts the legendary Chung K'uei and his sister on a demon hunt. Accompanied by a retinue of grotesque slave-demons, who carry Chung K'uei's sword, bundles of household goods and pots of wine, the demon-queller and his sister ride in sedan-chairs. The artist used dry-brush strokes to define the figures, with occasional accents of black ink. Stylized insects decorate some of the textiles. In his colophon written at the end of the handscroll, by Sung Wu (1260–1340), a contemporary of Kung K'ai, mentions that the small black mountain sprites bound to the ends of poles were pressed to make wine and minced to make demon pickle.

Although demons or grotesque creatures frequently appear in Buddhist paintings, few early examples of scrolls depicting demons alone are extant. Twenty-two colophons, ranging in date from the 14th to the 19th century, follow that of Kung K'ai. (The complete composition is reproduced on page 161.)

44 WIND AND SNOW IN THE FIR-PINES   61.34
by Li Shan (active late 12th century)
Ink and color on silk; height, 29.7 cm. (11 11/16 in.); length, 79.2 cm. (31 3/16 in.)

Chin dynasty
Gift of Mr. and Mrs. Eugene Meyer

Li Shan, who worked during the Chin dynasty, is usually classified as a follower of the Kuo Hsi tradition. This short handscroll depicts a scholar seated beside a brazier in a small thatched cottage surrounded by tall fir-pines. The blunt, angular brushstrokes used in painting the pine needles and rough bark are echoed in the clusters of bamboo and flowing stream. Li Shan's signature and seal appear at the beginning of the handscroll. Attached to the end of the scroll is a colophon written by Wang T'ing-yün (1151–1202).
(The complete composition is reproduced on page 161.)

45 A BREATH OF SPRING 31.1

by Tsou Fu-lei
Ink on paper; height, 34.1 cm. (13 7/16 in.); length, 223.4 cm. (188 in.)
Yüan dynasty

The handscroll, dated in correspondence with 1360, is one of the finest Chinese paintings of plum blossoms now extant. At the beginning of the painting, fresh shoots and delicate blossoms enframe a lichen-studded, gnarled old plum branch. The short, staccato brushstrokes become increasingly longer throughout the composition, culminating in the long, sweeping stroke that dramatically completes the plum branch. Aside from the information found in the inscriptions on this handscroll, apparently the only work by Tsou Fu-lei to survive, nothing is known of the Taoist artist. A long colophon written by Yang Wei-chen (1296–1370), dated in correspondence with August 27, 1361, appears at the end of the scroll.

46 CRABAPPLE AND GARDENIA 17.183

by Ch'ien Hsüan, ca. 1235–ca. 1300
Ink and color on paper; height, 29.2 cm. (11 1/2 in.); width, 78.3 cm.
(30 15/16 in.)
Yüan dynasty

These two small meticulously painted floral studies, originally part of an album, are now mounted as a short handscroll. The delicate color and sensitive outlines enhance the fragile beauty of the freshly opened blossoms. Ch'ien Hsüan's seal is affixed in the lower left corner of each painting. There is an inscription by Chao Meng-fu (1254–1322) on the mounting at the end of the painting. The handscroll formerly was in the collection of the noted Ch'ing dynasty collector, An Ch'i (ca. 1683-ca. 1744).
(The complete composition is reproduced on page 162.)

47 SHEEP AND GOAT 31.4

by Chao Meng-fu, 1254–1322
Ink on paper; height, 25.2 cm. (9 15/16 in.); width, 48.4 cm. (19 1/16 in.)
Yüan dynasty

A noted calligrapher, painter and statesman, Chao Meng-fu was one of the most important literati figures in the early years of the Yüan dynasty. Basing his composition on T'ang and Five Dynasties' models, Chao silhouetted the sheep and goat against the blank paper in tense counterpoise. In his inscription at the left of the scroll, Chao states that he painted the animals at the request of Chung-hsin. The seals of Ming and Ch'ing dynasty collectors, as well as an encomium and seals of the Ch'ien-lung Emperor are applied capriciously over most of the remaining paper.

48 MYRIAD BAMBOO 38.18

by Sung K'o, 1327–1387
Ink on paper; height, 24.9 cm. (9 13/16 in.); length, 98.1 cm. (38 5/8 in.)
Yüan dynasty

In China, bamboo symbolizes the gentleman who is able to maintain his own moral character regardless of outward change. Hence many literati artists specialized in painting ink bamboo. Sung K'o, who served as an official, was equally well-known as a poet and calligrapher. In this short handscroll, the lush bamboo is painted against a somewhat desiccated landscape established with long dry brushstrokes. Dark ink dabs occasionally accent the geometric shapes of the landscape, which are characteristic of Yüan dynasty painting. The artist's inscription is dated in correspondence with 1369.

(The complete composition is reproduced on page 162.)

49 FISHERMAN ON THE RIVER 30.80
by Tai Chin, 1388–1462
Ink and color on paper; height, 46.0 cm. (18 1/8 in.); length, 740.0 cm.
(291 3/8 in.)
Ming dynasty

Tai Chin served at the court briefly during the Hsüan-te period (1426–1435) before returning to his native Chekiang province. While he was influenced by the achievements of Southern Sung artists, Tai Chin's own ability to depict figures and landscapes with astonishingly swift brushstrokes established his reputation as founder of the Che school of painting. In this handscroll illustrating the activities of fishermen along a river, Tai Chin used bold, broad color washes reinforced with ink. The diagonal arrangement of the slender fishing boats throughout the composition increases the sense of animation suggested by the artist's daring brushwork.

(The complete composition is reproduced on pages 162 and 163.)

50 JOURNEY TO THE SOUTH 53.78
by T'ang Yin, 1470–1523
Ink on paper; weight, 24.3 cm. (9 9/16 in.); length, 89.3 cm. (35 3/16 in.)
Ming dynasty

T'ang Yin's reputation as a poet, painter and calligrapher is equalled only by the many stories found in Chinese literature describing his romantic exploits. A precocious student, his

162

chances for an official career were ruined when he was inadvertently linked with an examination scandal. Nonetheless, T'ang Yin was befriended by the outstanding literati of the day and emerged as one of the great artists of the Ming dynasty. In this short handscroll, the artist displays his ability to combine bold washes of dilute ink with delicately articulately details. An inscription by T'ang Yin is written at the end of the scroll. (The complete composition is reproduced above.)

51 CH'EN YÜAN-TA ADMONISHING LIU TS'UNG
  11.235

Ink and color on silk; width, 36.9 cm. (14 1/2 in.); length 207.9 cm. (81 7/8 in.)
Ming dynasty, 15th century

Narrative handscrolls depicting the exploits of meritorious ministers, loyal generals and paragons of filial piety, reflect the influence of the Confucian tradition. This painting represents a well-known historical incident dating from the fourth century A.D., in which the minister, Ch'en Yüan-ta, chained himself to a tree and admonished Liu Ts'ung, the ruler of the State of Han, who is shown here seated in the center of the composition, in slightly larger scale than the other figures. Only the courageous intervention of the Empress saved Ch'en from being carried away by the guards to be executed. The figures are drawn with strong outlines and washes of color. Texture strokes in ink appear only in the incidental landscape elements. The scroll, which formerly was in the Ch'ing dynasty Imperial collection, bears seals of the Chia-ch'ing Emperor (r. 1796–1820) and those of the noted collector, Liang Ch'ing-piao (1620–1691). There are colophons by Wang Chih-teng (1535–1612) and Han Feng-hsi (dated 1613).

(The complete composition is reproduced on page 164.)

52 BOAT MOORED BY A STORMY LAKE   11.162c

Ink and color on silk; height 25.8 cm. (10 3/16 in.); width, 27.6 cm. (10 7/8 in.)
Ming dynasty, 16 century

A man sits in his house under leafy trees on the shore of a lake watching his servants loading a boat. A horse and luggage cart suggest that he is about to begin a journey. The careful depiction of the waves, trees and rocks are similar to those works attributed to Chou Ch'en (active 1472–1535). This painting seems to be close to Chou Ch'en in time and style, possibly even his own work.

53 SCHOLAR'S ABODE IN THE MOUNTAINS   16.95

by Wang Shih-ch'ang
Ink and light color on silk; height, 184.2 cm. (72 1/2 in.); width, 101.7 cm. (40 1/16 in.)
Ming dynasty

Artists of the Che School often used the "three corner" compositions developed earlier by Southern Sung masters. In this painting, Wang Shih-ch'ang dramatically placed most of the landscape elements on the right side of the composition. Rather than leading the spectator progressively into deep space, as a Sung artist would have done, Wang Shih-ch'ang accented the mountain tops with bold, dark ink strokes, thereby bringing the forms into a more two-dimensional plane. Paintings by Wang Shih-ch'ang are relatively rare. Two large hanging scrolls in the National Palace Museum, Taiwan, are closely related in style to this painting. The artist's signature and seal appear in the upper left corner of the scroll.

54 LANDSCAPE IN THE STYLE OF LI T'ANG   39.4

by Ch'iu Ying, ca. 1510–ca. 1551
Ink and color on paper; height 25.4 cm. (10 in.); length, 306.7 cm. (120 3/4 in.)
Ming dynasty

The modest, tersely worded signatures usually found on Ch'iu Ying's paintings reveal a greater concern for painting than for poetry. A brilliant technical skill enabled Ch'iu Ying to interpret the work of earlier artists admired by Ming dynasty collectors. Here, according to the inscription, Ch'iu Ying is working in the style of the Sung dynasty artist, Li T'ang. The gnarled pines and roughly textured rocks are derived from the Li T'ang style, but the pastel washes of color and precise definition of individual details clearly are Ch'iu Ying's own contribution.

(The complete composition is reproduced on page 165.)

55 LANDSCAPE IN THE STYLE OF CHÜ-JAN   62.29

by Wang Shih-min, 1592–1680
Ink and color on paper; height, 27.0 cm. (10 5/8 in.); width, 37.1 cm. (15 5/8 in.)
Ch'ing dynasty

Wang Shih-min was a wealthy official, collector and connoisseur, as well as a gifted artist. By diligently studying and copying the works of ancient masters in his private collection, Wang Shih-min attained a sound understanding of past traditions. In six of these album leaves, now mounted as a handscroll, Wang Shih-min presents his own variations on the painting styles of six different artists. The name of the artist whose work formed the basis of the painting is duly presented above Wang Shih-min's seal on each album leaf. His inscription on the seventh and final leaf is dated in correspondence with 1670.

(All six of the paintings are reproduced on page 166.)

56 PEACH BLOSSOM SPRING 57.4

by Tao-chi, 1641–ca. 1717
Ink and color on paper; height, 25.0 cm. (9 7/8 in.); width, 157.8 cm.
 (62 1/4 in.)
Ch'ing dynasty

Tao-chi occupies a particularly important position among individualist painters of the Ch'ing dynasty. Reacting against popular academic painting styles of the period, Tao-chi sought a completely personal style that owed no debt to past traditions. In this handscroll illustrating T'ao Yüan-ming's (365–427) poem, the powerful application of ink and color reveal the strength of the artist's conception. Dabs of color and short, vibrato ink strokes imbue the small landscape with an extraordinary sense of monumentality. The fisherman, oar in hand, has just emerged from the cavern entrance to the lush valley where he is being met by three inhabitants of the fabled paradise.
(The complete composition is reproduced on page 167.)

57 DWELLING IN THE FU-CH'UN MOUNTAINS 50.19

by Wang Hui, 1632–1717

Ink and color on paper; height, 38.4 cm. (15 1/8 in.); width 743.5 cm.
 (293 3/4 in.)
Ch'ing dynasty

During the Ming and Ch'ing dynasty, the Yüan dynasty painter Huang Kung-wang (1269–1354) was universally venerated by literati artists. The most famous work by Huang Kung-wang is a long handscroll entitled, "Dwelling in the Fu-ch'un Mountains." Wang Hui's handscroll, based on the earlier composition, is especially important, since it preserves the beginning section now lost in the original Yüan painting. Wang Hui's own contribution was to imbue the robustness of the Yüan landscape with a new, undulating rhythm. An inscription at the end of the scroll by Wang Shih-min (1592–1680), Wang Hui's teacher, is dated in correspondence with 1673.
(The complete composition is reproduced on pages 168 and 169.)

58 LANDSCAPE IN THE STYLE OF HUANG KUNG-
WANG 62.5

by Wang Yüan-ch'i, 1642–1715
Ink and color on paper; height, 97.7 cm. (38 1/2 in.); width, 59.2 cm.
 (23 5/16 in.)
Ch'ing dynasty

Wang Yüan-ch'i was the youngest of the famous "Four Wangs," whose achievements dominated literati painting during the early years of the Ch'ing dynasty. A scholar and official, as well as a painter, Wang Yüan-ch'i's work displays an extremely intellectual approach to the interpretation of past traditions. Here he is working in the style of the Yüan dynasty master, Huang Kung-wang (1269–1354). While an occasional motif recalls the work of the earlier artist, the painstakingly assembled composition, seemingly built up of innumerable carefully designed units, ultimately is Wang Yüan-ch'i's own

creation. The artist's inscription is dated in correspondence with 1706.

59 MOUNTAIN AND RIVER LANDSCAPE 16.552

Anonymous

Hanging scroll; ink on silk; height, 163.6 cm. (64 7/16 in.); width, 107.2 cm.
  (42 3/16 in.)

Chin dynasty, 13th century

Following the collapse of the Northern Sung dynasty in 1126, most of northern China remained under the control of the Chin invaders for slightly more than a century. Paintings by artists working in north China during this period tended to continue Northern Sung traditions. In reworking earlier compositional elements and artistic traditions, Chin artists often produced paintings that betray exaggerations as well as simplifications of the original prototypes. This hanging scroll, formerly attributed to the Chin artist Li Shan, has been extensivly retouched.

Nonetheless, the curiously shaped rocks of the mountain and the downward-swept branches of the foreground trees retain much of their original character. The mist-shrouded mountains in the upper right corner of the paintings are somewhat different in mood, reflecting perhaps the eclecticism of the artist.

60 YANG KUEI-FEI MOUNTING A HORSE 57.14

by Ch'ien Hsüan, ca. 1235–ca. 1300

Handscroll; ink and color on paper; height, 29.5 cm. (11 5/8 in.); length,
  (117.0 cm. (42 1/8 in.)

Yüan dynasty

During the early years of the Yüan dynasty, artists like Ch'ien Hsüan revived ancient styles and fused them with their own innovations to create a new and viable artistic vocabulary. In subject matter, the T'ang dynasty Emperor Ming-huang (r. 713–756) astride a horse watching his favorite concubine, Yang Kuei-fei, being helped onto her saddle by maidservants and

attendants, is an obvious reference to the past. Ch'ien Hsüan's use of precise outline and flat color, as well as his arrangement of the figures against a blank background, reflect his awareness of the earlier achievements of T'ang dynasty artists. But a new sense of detached restraint which pervades the painting is typical of Ch'ien Hsüan's work and characteristic of Yüan dynasty archaism in general. There is an inscription by the artist at the end of the handscroll.

(The complete composition is reproduced on page 170.)

61 HORSE AND GROOM   45.32

by Chao Yung, born 1289
Handscroll; ink and color on paper; height, 31.7 cm. (12 1/2 in.); length, 73.5 cm.
  (28 15/16 in.)
Yüan dynasty, dated 1347

The achievement of the Northern Sung figure painting master, Li Kung-lin (1040–1106), exerted great influence on literati painting during succeeding dynasties. One of the most famous of Li Kung-lin's paintings was the "Five Horses", depicting five horses that had been presented to the Sung emperor as tribute between 1086 and 1088. In this short handscroll, Chao Yung, son of the famous Yüan dynasty artist, Chao Meng-fu (1254–1322), has copied one of the five horses from Li Kung-lin's painting. In contrast to the austere ink drawing of Li Kung-lin, Chao Yung has applied color to the foreign groom and the dappled horse. Chao Yung's inscription is dated in correspondence with 1347. Following the painting is a colophon by Wu K'uan (1435–1504).

62 BAMBOO IN THE WIND   53.85

by Wu Chen, 1280–1354
Hanging scroll; ink on paper; height, 109.0 cm. (42 15/16 in.); width, 32.6 cm.
  (12 13/16 in.)
Yüan dynasty, dated 1350

Three columns of calligraphy complement the single spray

of windblown bamboo. The inscription, dated in correspondence with 1350, states that Wu Chen painted the bamboo after seeing a stone engraving of a similar painting done by the Sung artist Su Tung-p'o (1036–1101). The arch of the bamboo stem, which culminates in the taut curve at the extreme upper section, is emphasized by the repetition of blade-like strokes to indicate leaves.

63 SECLUDED DWELLINGS IN THE SUMMER MOUNTAINS   59.17

by Wang Meng, ca. 1309–1385
Hanging scroll; ink on silk; height, 56.8 cm. (22 3/8 in.); width, 34.2 cm.
  (13 1/2 in.)
Yüan dynasty, dated 1354

The single figure crossing a bridge in the lower right leads the spectator into the composition, which progresses in a continous ground plane to the single massif dominating the upper center of the painting. Fine dry brush strokes define the rounded mountain forms and darker dabs of ink accent the landscape. A concern for rich textures and undulating movement is characteristic of Wang Meng's landscapes. According to his inscription in the upper left corner, Wang Meng did the painting for one Chung-fang in 1354.

64 DEVA KING   11.313

Anonymous
Hanging scroll; ink on silk; height, 127.3 cm. (50 1/8 in.); width, 44.2 cm.
  (17 3/8 in.)
Yüan dynasty, 14th century

Buddhist painting continued to flourish during the Yüan dynasty, although the names of only a few artist are still recorded. This hanging scroll, depicting a heavily armored deva king, perpetuates a tradition that is derived ultimately from the now-lost wall paintings of the T'ang master, Wu Tao-tzu (active 720–760). As is typical of later, smaller scale representations of Buddhist deities, the artist contrasts various intricate textile and metal patterns. The swirling drapery enhances the sense of imminent movement.

65 THE YÜEH-YANG TOWER   15.36i

By Hsia Yung, active 1340's
Album leaf; ink on silk; height, 26.2 cm. (10 5/16 in.); width, 26.7 cm. (10 1/2 in.)
Yüan dynasty, mid 14th century

Erected in the T'ang dynasty, the Yüeh-yang Tower in Hunan province commanded a superb view of Lake Tung-t'ing. It was repaired in 1045 and immortalized by Fan Chung-yen (989–1052) in his famous essay, the *Yüeh-yang-lou chi*. The text of the essay was transcribed onto the painting in minute characters by the artist, whose seal appears to the left of the inscription. The same predilection for the small scale is evident in the extremely meticulous rendering of the tower. In spite of the artist's concern for fine details and the utmost care he took to depict them, the painting is not in the least wooden. This is due in part to the relatively loose treatment of the rocks in the foreground and of the hills in the distance. Hsia Yung specialized in architectural paintings of this type, called *chieh hua* (boundary painting), and several other of his paintings of famous buildings are extant.

66 MOUNTAIN SCENERY ON THE WAY TO LIN-AN   64.2

by Liu Chüeh, 1410–1472
Handscroll; ink on paper; height, 33.6 cm. (13 1/4 in.); width, 57.8 cm. (22 3/4 in.)
Ming dynasty

This painting is a memento of a trip to Lin-an (Hangchow) in 1471 on which Liu Chüeh was accompanied by the artist Shen Chou (1427–1509), his younger brother, Shen Chao, and Shih Chien (1434–1496). Liu Chüeh actually did the painting for Shen Chao. There are six inscriptions in verse on the top of the painting. On a separate sheet, mounted after the painting, is a colophon by P'eng Nien (1505–1566). Even though the land-

scape supposedly refers to a specific site, the casual application of ink in short, staccato strokes reveals the artist's basic concern for informal, personal expression.

67 THE RED CLIFF   39.1

by Wen Cheng-ming, 1470–1559
Handscroll; ink and light color on paper; height, 30.5 cm. (12 in.); length, 141.5 cm. (55 3/4 in.)
Ming dynasty

The two Odes on the Red Cliff, written by the Sung dynasty poet-painter, Su Tung-p'o (1036–1101), have been a favorite subject for literati artists throughout succeeding centuries. In this handscroll, the tiny boat and three travelers moving swiftly over the wide expanse of water provide the focal point on the composition. The poet's black hat establishes an accent that is echoed by a few spare ink strokes applied over the light washes of color in the craggy mountains. Wen Cheng-ming wrote the title at the beginning of the handscroll; following the painting he also added the text of the two Odes and appended the date 1552, when he was 83 years old.
(The complete composition is reproduced on page 170.)

68 AUTUMN COLORS AT HSÜN-YANG   39.3

by Lu Chih, 1495–1576
Handscroll; ink and light color on paper; height, 22.3 cm. (8 3/4 in.); length, 100.1 cm. (39 7/16 in.)
Ming dynasty, dated 1554

Using delicate washes of color, with an occasional accent in darker ink, Lu Chih evokes the poignant scene described in Po Chü-i's (772–846) poem entitled *P'i-p'a-hsing*, "The Lute Song." The two small foreground boats, brushed by the same breeze that bends the river grasses, serve as the focal point in the famous story of the meeting of the poet and the aging courtesan. The refinement of brushwork and sensitive interpretation of the poem are characteristic of Lu Chih's paintings. The artist's inscription is dated in correspondence with 1554. P'eng Nien (1505–1566) wrote the title at the beginning of the handscroll;

the text of Po Chü-i's poem, written by Wen P'eng (1498–1573) is attached at the end of the handscroll.

(The complete composition is reproduced on page 171.)

69 APRICOT BLOSSOMS   54.8

by Hsü Wei, 1520–1593

Handscroll; ink on paper; height, 32.5 cm. (12 13/16 in.); length, 535.5 cm. (210 7/8 in.)
Ming dynasty

The swift, somewhat frenetic use of brush and ink in depicting the twelve plant studies in this handscroll reflects a similar impetuousness in the accompanying calligraphy. Hsü Wei is

said to have been extremely erratic in temperament and it is tempting to look for some reflection of his personality in his work. Violent outbursts of temper, one of which is said to have resulted in the death of his wife, seem to have alienated the artist from his contemporaries.

(The complete composition is reproduced on page 171.)

70 LANDSCAPE WITH FIGURE   61.10h

by Ch'en Hung-shou, 1599–1652
Album leaf; ink and color on paper; height 33.5 cm. (13 1/4 in.); width, 27.3 cm.
  (10 3/4 in.)
Ming dynasty

Although Ch'en Hung-shou's earlier work is characterized by an outspoken eccentricity, his later paintings are more gentle, even subdued in mood. In this album leaf, the solitary seated scholar, full-faced and clothed in billowing robes which hark back to T'ang dynasty conventions, is enframed by the barren trees and the rocks along the edge of a stream. The artist used a dry brush to articulate rocks, trees and water; with almost painstaking care he defined the tree branches and creepers. A mature, introspective mood pervades the small album leaf.

71 WINTER LANDSCAPE   61.11

by Kung Hsien, ca. 1617–1689
Album leaf; ink on paper; height, 20.5 cm. (8 1/16 in.); width, 34.0 cm.
  (13 3/8 in.)
Ch'ing dynasty

Kung Hsien was the most prominent member of the "Eight Masters of Nanking", who were active during the 17th century. Like so many other painters of the period, Kung Hsien simplified his artistic vocabulary and experimented with it to achieve the greatest expressive potential. In this small landscape he works with surprisingly few compositional shapes and ink values, yet succeeds in attaining a luminous snowscape. Originally, this leaf probably was one of an album. Although there is no signature or date, the style is similar to those works done during the late years of Kung Hsien's life.

72 PLUM BLOSSOMS   65.10

by Chin Nung, 1687–after 1764
Hanging scroll; ink and color on paper; height, 130.2 cm. (51 1/4 in.); width,
  28.2 cm. (11 1/8 in.)
Ch'ing dynasty, dated 1759

According to the inscription, Chin Nung did this painting as a present for a certain Mr. Ho-t'ing. The artist also states in his inscription that five years earlier he had done another painting of plum blossoms and inscribed an identical poem for Mr. Shen of Hua-t'ing, to felicitate him on the occasion of his acquiring a new concubine. Chin Nung wrote the inscription in the *pa-fen* style of the *li* script that usually is associated with his name. He developed this particular style of calligraphy after studying rubbings made from inscriptions on ancient stele. The attenuated branches are placed around the columns of calligraphy to complete the simple composition. Apparently the artist was more concerned with the visual pattern formed by the branches and blossoms than with any mere depiction of a realistic image.

73 SEATED BUDDHA   11.121

Height, 29.3 cm. (11 9/16 in.); width, 13.2 cm. (5 3/16 in.)
Six Dynasties, dated A.D. 451

The small gilt bronze Buddha figure, made during the Liu-Sung dynasty, provides an example of Chinese adaptation of the type of meditating Buddha that first appeared in Gandhara. The treatment of the facial features and drapery folds is more formalized and abstract than the Gandharan prototypes; the head is disproportionately large and the pleats of the robe have been reduced to symmetrically arranged parallel ridges. Three tiny seated Buddhas and kidney-shaped patterns decorate the halo, while a flaming aureole has been added to the outer edge.

74 GRAY LIMESTONE BODHISATTVA   52.15

Height, 103.4 cm. (40 11/16 in.); width, 41.7 cm. (16 7/16 in.)
Northern Wei dynasty, early 6th century A.D.

The Bodhisattva, probably Maitreya, carries a bottle in the left hand and a lotus-bud in the right. The dynamic silhouette formed by the broad, flat scarves and billowing hem contrasts with the calm, introspective expression on the face of the Bodhisattva. Some indication of the deeply felt faith that characterized early Chinese Buddhist sculpture is evident in the slightly archaic smile which lends a friendly, yet serene quality to the face of the youthful deity. Close similarities with Bodhisattva figures in the Buddhist caves at Kung-hsien, a site in Honan province, suggest a possible provenance for the statue.

(The complete section of the couch is reproduced on page 172.)

75 WHITE MARBLE BODHISATTVA SEATED IN
MEDITATION   11.411

Height, 33.0 cm. (13 in.); width, 17.5 cm. (6 7/8 in.)
Northern Ch'i dynasty, 550–577 A.D.

The bodhisattva is seated in the *lalitā-sana* position, with one
hand raised to the chin, the other placed across the left knee.
The head, framed by an intricately carved halo, is slightly in-
clined forward with eyes closed, as if deep in meditation. Only
the swirling lines of the stylized drapery folds contrast with the
serene stillness which pervades the figure. Broad, simply modelled planes of face and torso, heightened by contrast with the
exquisite details of interlaced tree branches, halo, diadem,
necklace and bracelets, are characteristic features of Northern
Ch'i sculpture. Three sides of the rectangular base depict a lotus
pond with adoring figures emerging from lotus blossoms. The

precise bas-relief details of lotus leaves, fish, ducks and figures are juxtaposed against an incised wave pattern.

76 GRAY LIMESTONE FUNERARY COUCH

15.109, 15.110, 15.336

Height, 60.0 cm. (23 3/4 in.); length, 234.0 cm. (92 in.)
Northern Ch'i dynasty, A.D. 550–577

The bas-relief decoration which completely covers the surface of the funerary couch is particularly important because of the unusual juxtaposition of Chinese and Persian elements. An elaborate incense burner in the center of the composition is flanked on either side by kneeling figures holding flaming jewels and guardians grasping tridents while trampling on lions. These details, in typical Northern Ch'i style, all are executed in high relief. By contrast, the figures of dancers and musicians, in roundels encircled by squares, are strongly Persian in costume and pose.

(The related figure is reproduced on page 172.)

77 GRAY LIMESTONE DEMON FIGURE   53.86

Height, 80.5 cm. (31 11/16 in.); width, 55.7 cm. (21 3/4 in.)
Northern Ch'i dynasty, 550–577 A.D.

Seated demon figures of this same type occur as caryatids in

the Buddhist caves at Southern Hsiang-t'ang-shan in Hopei province. While the carving of the monster mask, wings and sharp talons undoubtedly were meant to evoke a sense of awe in the spectator, the sculptor seems to have tempered the image with a slight suggestion of impious humor.

78 LIMESTONE BAS-RELIEF, THE PARADISE OF AMITABHA   21.2

Height, 158.9 cm. (62 1/2 in.); length, 334.5 cm. (131 3/4 in.)
Northern Ch'i dynasty, A.D. 550–577

This relief is supposed to have come from a cave in Southern Hsiang-t'ang-shan, a site located in Hopei province. Amitabha Buddha is seated before a pond welcoming those beings just emerging from lotus blossoms after having been newly-born into the Western Paradise. The monumental figures of the Buddha, Bodhisattvas and attendants are executed in simple, geometrical forms, which contrast with the sumptuously ornate canopy and stylized trees. All elements of the composition are arranged in successive stages with some areas deeply undercut so as to create an integrated pictorial unity. Some traces of pigment still remain on the surface of the stone, giving a faint indication of the brilliant vision that would have been seen by faithful Buddhist pilgrims who visited the cave temples.

79 BUDDHA   23.15

Height, 176.0 cm. (69 1/4 in.); width, 63.5 cm. (25 in.)
Sui dynasty, A.D. 581–618

The monumental marble Buddha image, completely clothed in a closely fitting monastic robe, is treated as a simple, monolithic form. This simplicity of form, with but the slightest indication of a physical body beneath the garments, is typical of Sui dynasty sculpture. Buddhist scenes, arranged in registers, cover both the front and back of the figure as if the sculptor had reproduced in stone some elaborately embroidered religious vestment. A comparison of the iconography with similar examples, both in sculpture and painting, enables us to identify the figure as Vairocana.

(Rubbings of the front and back are reproduced on page 173.)

80 BODHISATTVA   11.34

Height, 23.4 cm. (19 3/16 in.); width, 16.2 cm. (6 3/8 in.)
T'ang dynasty

The Bodhisattva, probably Kuan-yin, is depicted with full cheeks, small full lips and high arched eyebrows. The carefully plaited locks of hair, which fall over the Bodhisattva's shoulders, are held in place by a jeweled headband. Unfortunately, the topmost section of the headdress, which originally may have

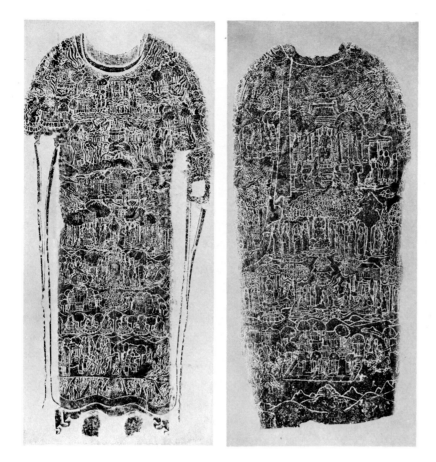

included a miniature representation of Amitabha, is broken. The graceful, slightly sensual modelling of the bejeweled torso is typical of T'ang dynasty Buddhist sculpture.

81 BODHISATTVA 16.365
Height, 101.7 cm. (16 1/8 in.); width, 40.9 cm. (16 1/8 in.)
T'ang dynasty

The lithe, muscular bodies and dramatic movement which characterize Buddhist images made during the early years of the T'ang dynasty reflect the influence of the Gupta renaissance in India. This Bodhisattva image is clothed in diaphanous robes with strands of jewelry hanging from the neck. The curving lines of the jewelry are repeated in the sharp edges of the drapery folds which are arranged in regular patterns. Although the contrasting diagonal planes of the body and the drapery folds imply imminent movement, the figure is meant to be seen from the front or back rather than from either side.

82 ELEVEN-HEADED KUAN-YIN, EKADASĀMUKHA-AVALOKITESVARA 09.98
Height, 100.8 cm. (39 11/16 in.); width, 31.7 cm. (12 1/2 in.)
T'ang dynasty, 8th century

This limestone form of Kuan-yin, the Bodhisattva of Mercy, is connected with Tantric worship. The ten additional small heads, symbolizing the ten stages on the way to enlightenment, are arranged on the Bodhisattva's headdress. Standing within the confines of a shallow niche, the full, sensual body of the Bodhisattva is clothed in diaphanous draperies and bedecked with meticulously carved jewelry. The sophisticated linear design of the floral halo and flying figures echoes the delicate tracery of the Bodhisattva's costume.

The figure is quite similar to another Eleven-headed Kuan-yin in the collection, which was commissioned as part of an elaborate sculptural decoration for the Kuang-chai Temple in Ch'ang-an, Shensi province. Some of the sculpture in the group bear dates ranging from 703 to 724. The close resemblance between the two Bodhisattvas in the Freer collection supports an early 8th century date for both figures.

(The related figure is reproduced on page 173.)

83 SEATED BUDDHA 44.46
Dry lacquer
Height, 99.5 cm. (39 1/16 in.); width, 72.5 cm. (28 9/16 in.)
Sung dynasty, 12th–13th century

Although this figure depicts Sakyamuni, the individualized treatment of the face, as well as the careful articulation on the body beneath the drapery folds, suggests that the artist actually produced the portrait of a Buddhist monk. During the Liao and Sung dynasties, many dry lacquer portraits of similar quality were produced in China. In the dry lacquer technique, layers of silk or hemp, soaked in lacquer, were spread over a clay core. When the lacquer had dried thoroughly, the sculptor would remove the clay core, leaving only the light, durable exterior. Some traces of polychrome still remain on the surface of the statue.

84 SEATED BODHISATTVA 45.4
Dry lacquer
Height, 58.3 cm. (22 15/16 in.); width, 43.1 cm. (17 in.)
Yüan dynasty, 13th century

The general treatment of this dry-lacquer figure, smooth and well filled out yet slim and vigorous; the almost heart-shaped face with finely cut nose, eyebrows and mouth; the sensitive and beautifully articulated hands, and the simple rope-like chignon are not in the Chinese tradition of the period. Such details have close parallels among 13th century Nepalese Tantric Buddhist images, however, and the marked Nepalese feeling in the modelling of the figure is, no doubt, a reflection of direct cultural exchange between the two countries. Esoteric Buddhism enjoyed Imperial support during the Yüan dynasty. The Mongols brought Lamaism to China, and it was this form of Buddhism that was encouraged by Kublai Khan under the influence of the celebrated lama 'Phags-pa.

85 WHITE EARTHENWARE JAR 39.42
Height, 33.2 cm. (13 1/16 in.); diameter, 28.3 cm. (11 1/8 in.)
Shang dynasty

White ware made in China during the Shang dynasty has such a fine texture that it occasionally is mistaken for porcelain; but analysis has shown that although the clay used is related to kaolin and contains much the same elements as does porcelain, it lacks the necessary vitreosity to produce a porcelain ware. The incised ornamentation which covers this entire vessel clearly is related to designs on contemporary bronze ritual vessels. A narrow band of four monoculi is applied on the shoulder, while the sides of the jar are covered with alternating plain and decorated chevron bands. Two pierced animal-headed lugs occur on the shoulder and a single pierced lug near the front base. The vase is one one of the best preserved examples of Shang dynasty white pottery ware known.

86 BLACK-GLAZED YÜEH WARE EWER   56.30

Height, 23.5 cm. (9 1/4 in.); width, 11.6 cm. (6 1/2 in.)
Six Dynasties, ca. 5th century A.D.

The ewer has a full swelling body, narrow neck and flaring mouth with a vertical lip. The short spout is decorated with a moulded chicken head; the dragon-headed handle curves to meet the lip. There are two lugs on the shoulder. The thick, oily black glaze, with olive green areas where thin, is covered with a fine overall crackle. Shards of similar black-glazed Yüeh ware were found at a kiln site near Te-ch'ing, about 25 miles north of Hangchow. This kiln may be the earliest Yüeh site so far discovered. Ewers of this type are extremely rare, providing examples of the earliest types of oriental stoneware with a high-fired black glaze.

87 WHITE PORCELAIN EWER   17.404

Height, 15.1 cm. (5 15/16 in.); width, 12.1 cm. (4 3/4 in.)
T'ang dynasty

The full, oval form of the ewer, the modeling of the lion-shaped handle and the treatment of the foot all support a T'ang dynasty date. A number of similar pieces are known, although only this example has a metal strip covering the lip. Probably the original neck was refashioned because of a break, and the present shape is the result. The white porcelain body is covered with a transparent white glaze.

88 EARTHENWARE JAR   30.32

Height, 59.8 cm. (23 9/16 in.); diameter, 46.0 cm. (18 1/8 in.)
T'ang dynasty

The unusually large ovoid body has a tall flaring neck, rounded lip and flat base. Relief medallions of alternating lion-head masks and floral designs are applied to the shoulder of the jar. Eight eyelets are placed between the medallions directly beneath eight smaller bosses. Three lines lightly incised on the shoulder of the jar probably were used as a guide in affixing the medallions and eyelets. The entire jar is covered with a green lead glaze with large areas of silvery iridescence. The swelling, vigorous lines of the vessel reflect a vitality characteristic of T'ang dynasty ceramics.

89 LUNG-CH'ÜAN VASE   37.18

Height, 25.9 cm. (10 3/16 in.); diameter, 11.3 cm. (4 7/16 in.)
Sung dynasty

Lung-ch'üan ware was manufactured at a number of kilns in Chekiang province during the Sung, Yüan and Ming dynasties; the name Lung-ch'üan is a type name rather than a precise identification of a particular kiln site. Large quantities of the ware were exported as early as the Sung dynasty, while even greater numbers were shipped to Japan, the Philippines, the Malay States and Western Asia during the Yüan and Ming dynasties. This *kinuta*, or mallet-shaped vase, with moulded fish handles and wide everted lip, is covered with a lustrous celadon glaze. The close-textured, unctuous surface, so reminiscent of jade,

makes it one of the finest of Sung dynasty monochrome glazes.

90 NORTHERN CELADON VASE   19.90

Height, 23.2 cm. (9 1/8 in.); diameter, 12.3 cm. (4 7/8 in.)
Sung dynasty

This pear-shaped vase has an everted lip and bold foot. The main body of the vase is decorated with incised foliate designs enclosing large, leafy forms. Double petals are incised along the vase. Another band of double petals on the neck is bordered above and below by simple foliate designs. Northern Celadon and Yüeh wares are closely related, their forms and carved designs often being quite similar, but the dark olive-green glaze of Northern Celadon ware differs from the paler glaze of Yüeh ware. The depth and vigor of the carved decoration on Northern Celadon ware, as seen in this vase, are different from all contemporary wares.

91 CHÜN WARE VASE   49.12

Height, 34.4 cm. (13 9/16 in.); diameter, 14.3 cm. (5 11/16 in.)
Yüan dynasty

Chün wares usually consist of a hard, fine-grained body covered with a thick coat of feldspathic glaze saturated with iron and made opaque with phosphates and Chinese clay. The blue-gray color of the glaze was produced by the presence of iron in a reducing kiln atmosphere, with a few red flambé spots accidentally or purposely caused by copper locally in the glaze. This vase has a pear-shaped body, a tall, slender, slightly flaring neck and a slanting foot. The buff-colored clay and strong, thick foot both indicate a Yüan dynasty date.

92 TING WARE BOWL   63.16

Height, 04.8 cm. (1 7/8 in.); diameter, 21.0 cm. (8 1/4 in.)
Sung dynasty

According to Chinese texts, fine white wares were being produced by the Imperial kilns at Ting-chou early in the Sung dynasty. Some potters from the Ting-chou kilns fled south with the court in 1127, establishing themselves in the district of Chi-chou in Kiangsi province. Some of the most beautiful wares from the Imperial Ting kilns were shallow bowls with wide flaring rims. These bowls were fired upside down, evidently to prevent warping, and the bare rims were often covered with a metal strip. On this bowl, two ducks and water plants are freely incised under the transparent glaze.

93 TING WARE VASE   59.6

Height, 16.3 cm. (6 7/16 in.); diameter, 16.6 cm. (6 1/2 in.)
Sung dynasty

The vase, of truncated bottle shape, has a flat base, rounded shoulder, short neck and flaring lip. Vases having this characteristic shape apparently date from the Northern Sung dynasty. The main body of the vase is decorated with foliate peony designs. Striated details scratched into the brown slip suggest the rather decorative veined pattern of leaves and petals. Double layers of petals are painted along the base of the vase. Ting ware of this type, with underglaze decoration in iron oxide, is relatively rare.

94 CHIEN WARE BOWL   09.369

Height, 08.8 cm. (3 1/2 in.); diameter, 19.2 cm. (7 9/16 in.)
Sung dynasty

Tea bowls of this type were made at Chien-ning in Fukien province. Although known as Chien ware in China, they are more commonly called Temmoku, the name given by Japanese who prized the ware for use in tea ceremonies. There are several variations in surface effect of this typical black and black-brown heavy viscous glaze. The Chinese describe this particular glaze as "oil spot" from the appearance of the iridescent flecks on the surface. There is a heavy roll where the glaze stops short of the foot. This example is unusual for its large size, the pristine condition of the glaze, and the flaring silhouette. The coarse reddish-black clay is fired hard.

95 TZ'U-CHOU WARE VASE   17.192
Height, 42.9 cm. (16 7/8 in.); diameter, 34.6 cm. (13 5/8 in.)
Sung dynasty

The large, ovoid shaped vase has a low, rounded shoulder and a small flanged neck. Lotus blossom designs, freely painted in brown, ornament the shoulder of the vase. A thick, glossy black glaze covers the entire buff stoneware body. The quality of clay and large, powerful potting suggest that the vase should be classified as Tz'u-chou ware, a stoneware first made during the Northern Sung dynasty. Although the ware originally was made in the Tz'u-chou district of modern Hopei province, it was also produced by many other kilns in other parts of China.

96 TZ'U-CHOU WARE VASE   31.18
Height, 39.7 cm. (15 5/8 in.); diameter, 20.6 cm. (8 1/8 in.)
Sung dynasty

The vase has a swelling shoulder, tall thin neck and widely flaring lip with a flanged edge. The hard, buff-colored stoneware was covered with a thick cream-colored slip and the decoration was then both incised in the slip and deeply cut through to expose the contrasting body color. Curving foliate bands, lightly incised, enframe the deeply cut band of swirling blossoms and leaves on the shoulder of the vase. Incised lotus panels ornament the foot. A thin, transparent glaze, now finely crackled, was applied over the slip before firing.

97 BLUE-AND-WHITE CANTEEN   58.2
Height, 47.5 cm. (18 3/4 in.); diameter, 41.8 cm. (16 7/16 in.)
Early Ming dynasty

This large circular canteen is an example of a form borrowed from an Islamic metal prototype by Chinese potters. There is no proper foot, and the canteen evidently was fired lying on its almost flat, unglazed back. Two large free-moving ring handles are attached to the shoulders by vertically placed annular lugs that are rectangular in section. The decoration, drawn in a strong cobalt blue, is essentially Chinese in character; both the style and execution serve to date the piece within the first third of the fifteenth century. Basically the conception is simple, in that the design consists almost entirely of waves and floral scrolls. Nonetheless, there are certain details that are not standard in the usual Chinese repertory. The distinctive wave pattern, which appears as a broad band on the lower zone of the neck, forms a broad circumferential border for the main surface and provides a surrounding background for the design on the central boss. The fine lines of the background water, against which the tossing whitecaps stand out in bold contrast, are arranged in smoothly undulating patterns to give the effect of rolling waves. Even more striking is the bold, geometric eight-pointed star that dominates the decoration of the central boss, reflecting a borrowing from a Near Eastern design.

98 BLUE-AND-WHITE DISH   61.14
Height, 09.5 cm. (3 3/4 in.); diameter, 68.0 cm. (26 3/4 in.)
Early Ming dynasty

This dish, exceptionally large in size and unusually well painted, displays the best qualities of a new, refined feeling for order that characterizes blue-and-white ware made during the early 15th century. The central scene is carefully planned with

a bit of land in the foreground and a body of water beyond into which juts a promontory in the background. Dominating the center of the scene is a garden rock beside which grows a tall coxcomb. This central group is flanked by two nightshades and two narcissus plants. In the foreground are two dandelions, and a knotweed grows on the distant promontory. Reading clockwise, the cavetto is decorated with sprays of peach, camellia, cherry, day lily, pomegranate, narcissus, pomegranate and chrysanthemum.

99 BLUE-AND-WHITE BOWL   52.4
Height, 09.5 cm. (3 3/4 in.); diameter, 20.4 cm. (9 1/16 in.)
Ming dynasty

The decoration inside the center of the bowl consists of pine, bamboo and plum—"the three friends of winter"—together with a formalized garden rock enclosed within double circles. The figures in the landscape on the outside of the bowl are separated by a pine, bamboo and tall stone. The unblemished, delicate, rather pale bluish-white porcelain body and the sure brushwork combine to make this bowl an extraordinarily fine example dating from the second half of the 15th century.

100 BLUE-AND-WHITE BOWL   53.75
Height, 12.3 cm. (4 7/8 in.); diameter, 28.0 cm. (11 in.)
Cheng-te period, A.D. 1506–1521, Ming dynasty

The inside of the bowl is decorated with a key fret border and in the center an Arabic inscription surrounded by scrolls. The phrase may be translated, "Thanks for his grace." On the outside there are six medallions with Arabic script amid floral motifs. These inscriptions, taken together, make a single sentence which may be translated, "May good luck and power of overlordship be perpetual which everyday are on the increase." Inscriptions of this kind are not unusual on early 16th century blue-and-white porcelain. There is a six-character Cheng-te mark on the base.

101 TOU-TS'AI STEM-CUP   51.16
Height, 08.0 cm. (3 1/8 in.); diameter, 06.3 cm. (2 1/2 in.)
Ch'eng-hua period, A.D. 1465–1487, Ming dynasty

The interior of the stem cup is decorated only with a single underglaze blue line around the rim. On the exterior, floral designs in underglaze blue and overglaze translucent enamel colors are arranged in formal groupings. The overlapping petal band which appears in the proper upright position around the bottom of the stem cup occasionally is seen on wares dating from the Ch'eng-hua period. A six-character Ch'eng-hua mark is written in a horizontal line under the glaze that partially covers the hollow foot.

102 KU-YÜEH-HSÜAN VASE   54.127
Height, 17.2 cm. (6 3/4 in.); diameter, 09.5 cm. (3 3/4 in.)
Ch'ien-lung period, 1736–1795 A.D., Ch'ing dynasty

The finest Ku-yüeh-hsüan porcelains made during the Ch'ien-lung period are characterized by white, glossy texture and delicate enamel decoration. This small vase with an "onion" shaped mouth is ornamented with a seated female figure and two children amusing themselves in a garden. An awareness of Western painting techniques is apparent in the modelling of the faces and hands. A ten-character poem stresses the transience of nature: "When branches put forth new shoots, the noon is at its zenith; when blossoms are at their fullest, autumn naturally has come." There is a four-character Ch'ien-lung mark in gray enamel on the base.

103 KU-YÜEH-HSÜAN BOWL   30.35

Height, 04.6 cm. (1 13/16 in.); diameter, 08.1 cm. (3 3/16 in.)
Yung-cheng period, A.D. 1723–1736, Ch'ing dynasty

Ku-yüeh-hsüan type porcelains made during the Yung-cheng period usually are considered to be of especially high quality. This small bowl is decorated in overglaze enamel colors with five mynah birds on an autumn branch and a ten-character inscription. There is a four-character Yung-cheng mark in dark gray-blue enamel on the base.

104 SILVER BOWL   31.8

Height, 05.5 cm. (2 3/16 in.); diameter, 14.5 cm. (5 11/16 in.)
T'ang dynasty, 8th century

Lotus shaped bowls of this type reflect Persian influence, both in form and ornamentation. Each petal is decorated with a symmetrical floral design raised on a ground of regular ring matting; the raised designs are gilded. A central ridge running vertically down the petals emphasizes the embossed technique. The petals, which stop short of the lip, give the impression of forming a separate stand for the bowl. Birds and animals enframed by plants ornament the outer edge of the flaring lip. There is a medallion in fire-gilt ornament on the base. The bowl is made of three silver pieces soldered together. The extraordinarily meticulous detail on this small bowl provides some indication of the high level of Chinese metal craftsmanship during the T'ang dynasty.

105 SILVER CUP   30.51

Height, 06.4 cm. (2 9/16 in.); diameter, 07.8 cm. (3 1/16 in.)
T'ang dynasty

Small cups with a handle frequently were made in silver during the T'ang dynasty. Similar examples in Persian silver suggest that these cups were based on foreign models. Contact with Persian silversmiths or Persian silver artifacts may well have stimulated Chinese craftsmen to make greater use of the metal during the T'ang dynasty. The designs on the flaring sides of the cup are divided into registers. Grape clusters and leaves framed by curvilinear tendrils, also a non-Chinese motif, border the main register where animals and birds move animatedly through more elaborate grape cluster and leaf designs. The handle is formed by a small "c" shaped ring partially covered by elongated leaves. The pattern, chased on a ground of regular ring matting, is covered with gilt.

106 GOLD APSARAS   46.20, 46.21

Height, 03.7 cm. (1 7/16 in.); length, 08.8 cm. (3 1/2 in.)
T'ang dynasty, 8th–9th century

This pair of apsaras, or Buddhist heavenly beings, is especially fine example of T'ang dynasty workmanship. Each

figure is made of sheet gold and the several parts soldered together. Gold streamers, ribbons and beaded ruffs are attached to the figures. The stylized curvilinear cloud formations on which the apsaras are borne aloft echo the fluttering lines of the floating scarves and streamers to imbue the figures with a sense of bouyant movement.

(Both apsaras are reproduced on page 176.)

107 SILVER COVERED BOX   30.39

Height, 06.4 cm. (2 9/16 in.); diameter, 05.0 cm. (2 in.)
T'ang dynasty, 8th–9th century

During the T'ang dynasty, under the influence of Western prototypes, Chinese artisans made extensive use of floral and fruit forms, both as shapes and ornamentation. This miniature covered box is modelled in the shape of an eight-lobed melon. Plain gold bands separate each section; grape clusters and leaves enclosed by curving vines ornament the various sections. The silver background of regular ring matting enhances the gilded surface of the elegantly worked design. The handle is modelled in the shape of a frog-like creature.

108 GOLD COVERED JAR   52.29

Height, 09.2 cm. (3 5/8 in.); diameter, 09.1 cm. (3 9/16 in.)
Ming dynasty, 15th century

This piece is one of a set of eight gold objects which were said to have come from the tomb of the Hsüan-te Emperor (r. 1426–1435). In addition to the incised pattern of dragons among clouds, there are a number of jewel settings or bezels symmetrically arranged on the jar and cover. These jewels include uncut rubies, sapphires and irregularly shaped pearls. The rather crude settings for the jewels appear un-Chinese and it has been suggested that the technique reflects foreign influence.

109 GOLD AND TURQUOISE JU-I   37.45

Length, 24.0 cm. (9 1/2 in.) exclusive of tassel
Ch'ien-lung period, 1736–1795 A.D., Ch'ing dynasty

This ju-i originally was included with eighteen gold objects designed for use on the Imperial desk, presented to the Ch'ien-lung Emperor by a Manchu official in 1783. The term ju-i, literally translated "as you wish", refers to a sceptre-like object often held by Manjusri when debating with Vimalakirti. This sceptre is fashioned of gold sheets and outlined at the corners by large beaded wire. The turquoise inlay is set in similar cloisonné settings, but the three large stones are set in repoussé-decorated bezels. The handle of the sceptre is decorated with the Eight Buddhist Emblems: the Wheel, Conch Shell, Umbrella, Canopy, Lotus, Vase, Paired Fish and the Endless Knot. Turquoise bats and peaches, symbolizing happiness and long life, adorn the larger end of the sceptre.

110 INCENSE BURNER   61.12

Height, 14.0 cm. (5 1/2 in.); diameter, 19.0 cm. (7 1/2 in.)
Ming dynasty, 16th century

During the sixteenth century, cloisonné incense burners based on ancient ritual bronze ting, or tripods, were one of the most common shapes. Usually the rim was plain; but often, as here, the simple rim was removed and replaced by a more elaborate rim cast during the Ch'ing dynasty. The fitted gilt feet also are later additions. The incense burner is covered with floral and fruit designs in red, white, blue, green, yellow and aubergine cloisonné enamels.

111 VASE   11.145

Height, 30.8 cm. (12 1/8 in.)
K'ang-hsi period, A.D. 1662–1722, Ch'ing dynasty

The vase is made in the shape of a Shang dynasty ceremonial *ku* vessel. Floral ornamentation with archaistic *t'ao-t'ieh* masks in light blue, dark blue, green, red, yellow and white cloisonné enamels decorate the surface. A separate pierced flower holder fits inside the mouth of the vase. An eight-character inscription cast in relief inside the foot rim states that the vase was made during the K'ang-hsi period by Wang Tzu-fan. Since cloisonné pieces with K'ang-hsi period marks are extremely rare, this vase is of importance in dating unmarked examples.

112 STEM CUP   49.1
Lacquer on wood; height, 23.5 cm. (9 1/4 in.); width, 17.9 cm.
(7 7/16 in.)
Chou dynasty, 5th–4th century B.C.

The stem cup was excavated at Ch'ang-sha in Hunan province, capital of the ancient state of Ch'u. Of remarkably large size, the stem cup is constructed in three separate pieces: cup, stem and base. Two pairs of highly stylized long-necked cranes decorate the wing-tipped handles, while a dragon ornaments the center of the inner surface of the cup. The black lacquer outer surfaces of the stem cup are decorated with geometric designs in shades of vermilion which are brighter than the geometric designs on the stem and base of the vessel. Comparison of the shape and ornamentation with similar pieces suggests that the stem cup dates from the 5th–4th century B.C.

113 BOWL   53.8
Lacquered fabric; height, 5.5 cm. (2 9/32 in.); diameter, 27.1 cm. (11 7/16 in.)
Chou dynasty, 5th–3rd century B.C.

Excavations at Ch'ang-sha in Hunan province have unearthed large numbers of lacquer objects dating from the late years of the Chou dynasty. These lacquer wares are characterized by careful workmanship and extremely sophisticated painted ornamentation. While most of the Ch'ang-sha lacquers are made over thin wood, this bowl has a fabric core. The tautly designed animal forms and geometric borders are skillfully applied in red and dull brown lacquer over a glossy brown lacquer ground.

114 LACQUER BOWL   68.67
Height, 03.5 cm. (1 3/8 in.); diameter, 22.0 cm. (8 5/8 in.)
Sung dynasty

The refined and simple shapes of Sung dynasty lacquer ware closely parallel those of porcelains dating from the same period. Completely unornamented, except for an occasional metal rim, the appeal of these lacquer pieces depends solely on their elegant form and rich, sober color. Recent archeological excavations have unearthed examples of lacquer ware together with related Sung dynasty artifacts, leaving little question as to the authenticity of their early date. This dish has a flattened foliate rim and matching cavetto fluting on both the inside and outside. There are occasional lighter areas and some crackle on the deep chocolate-brown lacquer.

115 COVERED BOX   53.64
Lacquered wood; height, 7.9 cm. (3 1/8 in.); diameter, 26.6 cm. (10 1/2 in.)
Yung-lo period A.D. 1403–1425, Ming dynasty

During the first half of the fifteenth century, special diaper backgrounds were used in Chinese carved lacquer ware to delineate air, water and land. A yellow lacquer ground and a distinctive layer of black lacquer were sometimes added beneath the upper layer of red lacquer as a guide to the carver. The detailed carving on the cover and sides of this box is typical of early 15th century carved lacquer and gives some indication of the extraordinary technical skill achieved by Chinese craftsmen.

116 STANDING BUDDHA   52.28
Gilt bronze; height, 35.9 cm. (14 1/8 in.); width, 14.4 cm. (5 11/16 in.)
Northern Wei dynasty, early 6th century

The Buddha stands on a lotus pedestal with the right hand in *abhaya mudrā* and the left in *vara mudrā*. The elongated facial features and elegant linear rhythms of the heavy drapery folds are characteristic of Northern Wei style. The removable mandorla is richly decorated with floral patterns and a flame border cast in low relief.

Although the bronze is uninscribed, comparison with dated examples of similar style suggests a date in the third or fourth decade of the sixth century.

117 STELE   69.5
Sandstone; height, 70.0 cm. (27 1/2 in.); width, 34.2 cm.
(13 1/2 in.)
Northern Wei Dynasty, dated April 29, 521

The stele is related to a group of similar Northern Wei pieces said to have come from Fu Hsien in Shensi province. Characteristic of these Fu Hsien reliefs is the reddish sandstone and fine linear articulation of forms. The full jowls, incised hair and eyebrows, and elongated earlobes are common features. The upper section of the stele, now lost, probably depicted two dragons and symbolic representations of sun and moon. These features are closely related to Taoist concepts and reflect the fusion of both Taoist and Buddhist ideas. The inscription, dated in correspondence with April 29, 521, states that the stele was

All eight pieces of the set shown in Plate 108.

carved by two monks, Liu Ta-ts'ang and Fa-tsun, for their younger brother.

118 BUDDHIST TRINITY 14.21

Gilt bronze; height, 32.1 cm. (12 5/8 in.); width, 14.1 cm. (5 9/16 in.)
Sui dynasty, A.D. 597

The three figures, Sakyamuni and two attendant Bodhisattvas, stand on a small dais decorated with scalloped edges and an incised inscription dated in correspondence with A.D. 597. The graceful lines of the scarves hanging from the Bodhisattva's headdresses and robes, together with the curvilinear foliate forms of the supporting brackets, contrast with the more simply clad, austere figure of Sakyamuni. The tilted plane of the three halos emphasizes the slightly forward bend of the heads and counterbalances corresponding curves in the chests and hips of the three figures. The measured, undulating grace that animates the Buddhist trinity is quite different from the more frenetic postures of Buddhist figures in the succeeding T'ang dynasty.

119 HEAD OF A GUARDIAN FIGURE 14.20

Limestone; height, 38.6 cm. (15 3/16 in.); width, 19.9 cm. (7 13/16 in.);
T'ang dynasty, early 8th century

The facial features, such as the curling lips, aquiline nose, protruding eyes and high, ornamental eyebrows, are carefully modelled and contribute to the expression of indomitable strength. The damaged top-knot as well as the condition of the stone at the back of the head suggest that it originally may have been part of a figure carved in high relief. A possible provenance for the head is provided by the hard, gray limestone, which is similar to that found in the Buddhist sanctuaries in the area of Lung-men, Honan province.

120 DISH 54.124

Earthenware with colored lead glazes; height 6.4 cm. (2 1/2 in.), diameter 28.5 cm. (11 1/4 in.)
T'ang dynasty, 618–907

T'ang dynasty pottery with colored glazes was probably influenced by Western or Near Eastern models both in form and decoration. The incised design and three low spreading feet on the dish seem to be derived from metal prototypes. The central design, depicting a goose flying amid three clouds, is surrounded by stylized lotus leaves alternating with foliate forms. The colors of the soft lead glazes, green, ochre and blue, are kept separated by the lines of the incised design. The rest of the interior is covered with a cream colored glaze which has developed iridescence. The glazes are finely crazed and has flaked in places. The exterior and the feet are unglazed.

121 BURIAL FIGURINE OF DANCER 49.27

Earthenware with three-color glazes; height 28.2 cm. (11 1/8 in.)
T'ang dynasty, 618–907

Music and dancing were among the pleasures enjoyed at the T'ang court and by the well-to-do, and the large numbers of musicians and dancers, often in sets, excavated from T'ang tombs are a clear indication of this. Our dancer wears a characteristic high headdress. The head and flesh areas are unglazed and bear faint traces of pigment. Three-color glazes of green, yellowish-brown and white cover the costume, the shoes, and the plaque on which the figure stands.

122 VASE 09.325

White porcelain with ivory white glaze; height 10.4 cm. (4 1/8 in.), greatest diameter 15.6 cm. (6 1/8 in.)
T'ang dynasty, 9th century

The vase was made in two parts: the depressed globular body on a broad low foot and the bowl-like upper portion complete with foot were thrown separately, joined, and a center opening made. An opaque lustrous ivory white glaze, stained in parts, covers the entire vase except for the base and foot, where the body is exposed. The relatively rough finish of the base and foot is typical of T'ang ceramics. White ware of this type was made in north China during the latter part of the T'ang dynasty and was the precursor of Ting ware of the Sung dynasty.

123 COVERED CONTAINER 44.12

Yüeh ware; stoneware with grayish green glaze; height 5.2 cm. (2 1/6 in.); diameter 13.7 cm. (5 7/16 in.)
Northern Sung dynasty, 10th century

Yüeh ware, named after the old principality at the mouth of the Yangtze, has a history reaching back to the 3rd or 4th century B.C. During the T'ang dynasty the ware was much refined and production continued into the earlier part of the Sung. This box has an everted foot, and the gray, hard body is covered with a grayish green celadon-type glaze. There are six elongated spur marks on the glazed base. The cover is ornamented with an all-over design of three flowers carved in low relief. The piece was probably made at Shang-lin hu, a kiln center in northern Chekiang about 45 miles east of Shao-hsing.

124 JAR 45.10

Stoneware with dark brown glaze; height 28.6 cm. (11 5/16 in.); diameter 27.6 cm. (10 7/8 in.)
Northern Sung dynasty, 11th century

This jar has a wide mouth and two strap handles. The stoneware body is covered with a dilute brown glaze. Closely spaced ribbings, running from the shoulder to two-thirds down the sides as well as on the handles, were applied. Covering the neck, the handles and the ribbed area is a lustrous dark brown glaze, under which the ribs appear lighter in color. The irregularity of the ribbing contributes to the vitality and power of this piece. Probably the product of a northern kiln, the jar purports to come from Ch'ing-ho in Hopei province which was submerged by flood early in the 12th century. Comparable shards recovered from the town lend support to the provenance and suggest the 11th century date.

125 VASE 19.95

Tz'u-chou ware; stoneware with colorless glaze; height 13.5 cm. (5 5/16 in.), diameter 14.8 cm. (5 13/16 in.)
Sung dynasty, 11th–12th century

Tz'u-chou ware, made in several localities in north China during the Sung dynasty, differs markedly from the so-called classical Sung wares. The Tz'u-chou potters brought to their craft a vigor and an inventiveness which make the ware the most varied and refreshing one of its time. A number of decorative techniques were developed, among them the *sgraffito*, exemplified in the vase here illustrated. The floral design was carved through the slip to the buff body underneath by cutting away the background. After glazing and firing, it shows up against the dark ground. The details are incised.

126 VASE 11.338

Kuan ware; height 23.2 cm. (9 1/8 in.); diameter 14.1 cm. (5 9/16 in.)
Southern Sung dynasty, 12th century

Kuan ware was the imperial ware of the Southern Sung dynasty, said to have been made at Phoenix Hill in the vicinity of the palace at Hangchow. This vase of outstanding quality has a barrel-shaped body and a tall, cylindrical neck with two encircling ridges. The thin paste is hard and dark, and is covered with a thick, lustrous, bluish-gray glaze with crackles.

127 STEM BOWL WITH COVER 68.77

Porcelain with underglaze blue decoration; height 13.3 cm (5 1/4 in.); diameter 9.8 cm. (3 7/8 in.)
Ming dynasty, reign of Hsüan-te (1426–1435)

Porcelain decorated with underglaze blue reached a peak of perfection during the reign of Hsüan-te. The decoration on the almost globular bowl consists of a continuous meander of star-shaped flowers with a band of zig-zags above and stylized vertical petals below. The petals are repeated around the splayed part of the stem along the edge of which is a ring of dots. The domed cover has larger petals radiating from a coin motif in the center from which a knob rises. An unusual feature is the occurrence of a floral motif enclosed by two concentric circles in the center of the interior. A six-character mark, "Ta Ming Hsüan-te nien chih", is written in blue on the main zone of ornamentation.

128 JAR 45.1

Fa-hua; height 30.5 cm. (12 in.), diameter 34.5 cm. (13 9/16 in.)
Ming dynasty, c. 1500

The jar is decorated in cloisonné style. After the body had been fired at porcelain temperature, the individual designs were outlined with threads of slip to separate the different colored lead-silicate glazes in much the same way as metal wires are used in cloisonné enamel. These glazes were then fired at a medium temperature. Detailed decoration is delicately incised.

The main body of the jar is decorated with herons, insects and crabs amid lotus blossoms and leaves. Stylized waves and rocks ornament the base, while a band of cloud collar points frame floral designs on the shoulder. Stylized cloud forms ornament the short neck of the jar. Medium fired opaque white, blue, turquoise, aubergine and brownish-yellow glazes are applied to the surface of the vessel.

129 VASE 47.16

Porcelain with blue crackled glaze; height 41.2 cm.
(16 3/16 in.); diameter 21.2 cm. (8 5/16 in.)
Ch'ing dynasty, reign of K'ang-hsi (1662–1722)

This vase, with globular body and tall, slender neck, is heavily potted and covered with a fine, lavender blue glaze with an even crackle. Monochrome porcelain made during the reign of K'ang-hsi is distinguished by a technical perfection matched by fine shape, beauty of color and texture of glaze, qualities which are admirably demonstrated by this vase.

130 VASE 41.2

Porcelain with celadon glaze; height 21.1 cm. (8 5/16 in.); diameter 8.5 cm.
(3 3/8 in.)
Ch'ing dynasty, reign of K'ang-hsi (1662–1722)

This vase, with ovoid body and tall neck with flaring lip, has a fine-grained, white porcelain body. A transparent, glossy pale green celadon glaze covers the entire vase except for the lip and the base which are glazed white. Round the lower portion of the vase is a row of stylized vertical petals in low relief. Between the petals the glaze is thicker and darker, providing a slight accent of color. A six-character mark, "Ta Ch'ing K'ang-hsi nien chih," is written in blue underneath the white glaze on the base. This piece is a conscious revival of the best of Lung-ch'üan celadon of the Sung dynasty, and achieves a cool flawlessness which can only be fully appreciated through touch.

131 COVERED LACQUER BOX 68.76

Height, 17.8 cm. (7 in.); diameter, 32.0 cm. (12 5/8 in.)
Ming dynasty, late 15th century

The cover of the circular box is delicately carved with a mythological scene depicting a group of figures assembled before the lunar palace of Ch'ang O. The three-legged toad climbing on the rocks in the lower left, as well as the hare pounding with mortar and pestle in the foreground are traditional symbols of the moon. On the curving sides of the cover are four rounded panels enclosing sages separated by *ch'i-lin* with clouds and fungus. Beneath vertical bands of scrolling lotus, the body of the box is decorated with figures, animals and floral designs. By contrasting the rounded brownish-black surface layer with the red diaper patterns and yellow ground, the artist achieved an unusually ornate surface pattern within a shallow depth. The artist, Wang Ming of P'ing-liang, inscribed his name on the right column of the left verandah. The same name appears on a lacquer dish dated 1489 in a private collection.
(A side view of the box is reproduced above.)

CHINESE CERAMICS

Prehistoric and Shang

Urn
Pottery with painted decoration
Yang-shao culture
C. 3000 B.C.

Ewer
Reddish pottery
Lung-shan culture
C. 2000 B.C.

Jar, type *li*
Gray pottery
Shang Dynasty
17th-13th century B.C.

Jar, type *lei*
White pottery
Shang Dynasty
13th-11th century B.C.

Basin
Pottery with gray glaze
Shang Dynasty
13th-11th century B.C.

Chou and Han

Jar, type *tsun*
Pottery with gray glaze
Western Chou Dynasty
10th-9th century B.C.

Covered jar
Pottery with colored glazes
Late Eastern Chou Dynasty
3rd century B.C.

Jar, type *hu*
Pottery with unfired painted decoration
Han Dynasty
2nd-1st century B.C.

Jar
Stoneware with gray glaze
Han Dynasty
1st century B.C.-1st century A.D.

Jar
Stoneware with green glaze
Han Dynasty
1st-2nd century A.D.

Han, Three Kingdoms period and Six Dynasties

Jar
Porcelain with green glaze
Han Dynasty
2nd century A.D.

Incense burner
Porcelain with green glaze
Western Chin Dynasty
3rd century

Ewer with chicken-headed spout
Porcelain with green glaze
Eastern Chin Dynasty
4th century

Vase with overall lotus petal motif
Porcelain with green glaze
Six Dynasties period
6th century

Jar with lotus petal motif
Porcelain with green glaze
Six Dynasties period
6th century

T'ang and Five Dynasties period

Phoenix-headed ewer
Porcelain with white glaze
T'ang Dynasty
7th-8th century

Jar
Porcelain with white glaze
T'ang Dynasty
7th-8th century

Jar
Pottery with three-colored glazes
T'ang Dynasty
8th century

Dish with foliated lip
Porcelain with white glaze
Five Dynasties period
10th century

Ewer
Porcelain with white glaze
Five Dynasties period
10th century

CHINESE CERAMICS

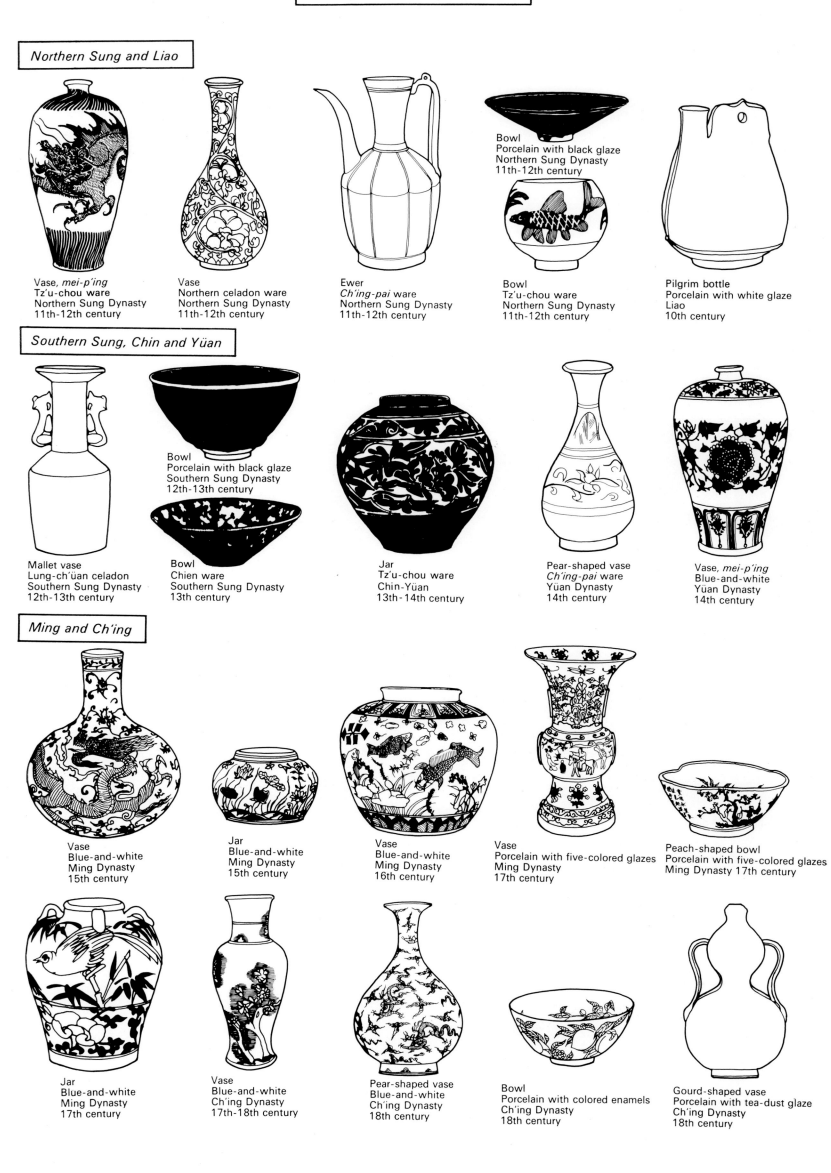

Northern Sung and Liao

Vase, *mei-p'ing*
Tz'u-chou ware
Northern Sung Dynasty
11th-12th century

Vase
Northern celadon ware
Northern Sung Dynasty
11th-12th century

Ewer
Ch'ing-pai ware
Northern Sung Dynasty
11th-12th century

Bowl
Porcelain with black glaze
Northern Sung Dynasty
11th-12th century

Bowl
Tz'u-chou ware
Northern Sung Dynasty
11th-12th century

Pilgrim bottle
Porcelain with white glaze
Liao
10th century

Southern Sung, Chin and Yüan

Mallet vase
Lung-ch'üan celadon
Southern Sung Dynasty
12th-13th century

Bowl
Porcelain with black glaze
Southern Sung Dynasty
12th-13th century

Bowl
Chien ware
Southern Sung Dynasty
13th century

Jar
Tz'u-chou ware
Chin-Yüan
13th-14th century

Pear-shaped vase
Ch'ing-pai ware
Yüan Dynasty
14th century

Vase, *mei-p'ing*
Blue-and-white
Yüan Dynasty
14th century

Ming and Ch'ing

Vase
Blue-and-white
Ming Dynasty
15th century

Jar
Blue-and-white
Ming Dynasty
15th century

Vase
Blue-and-white
Ming Dynasty
16th century

Vase
Porcelain with five-colored glazes
Ming Dynasty
17th century

Peach-shaped bowl
Porcelain with five-colored glazes
Ming Dynasty 17th century

Jar
Blue-and-white
Ming Dynasty
17th century

Vase
Blue-and-white
Ch'ing Dynasty
17th-18th century

Pear-shaped vase
Blue-and-white
Ch'ing Dynasty
18th century

Bowl
Porcelain with colored enamels
Ch'ing Dynasty
18th century

Gourd-shaped vase
Porcelain with tea-dust glaze
Ch'ing Dynasty
18th century

CHINESE BRONZE VESSELS

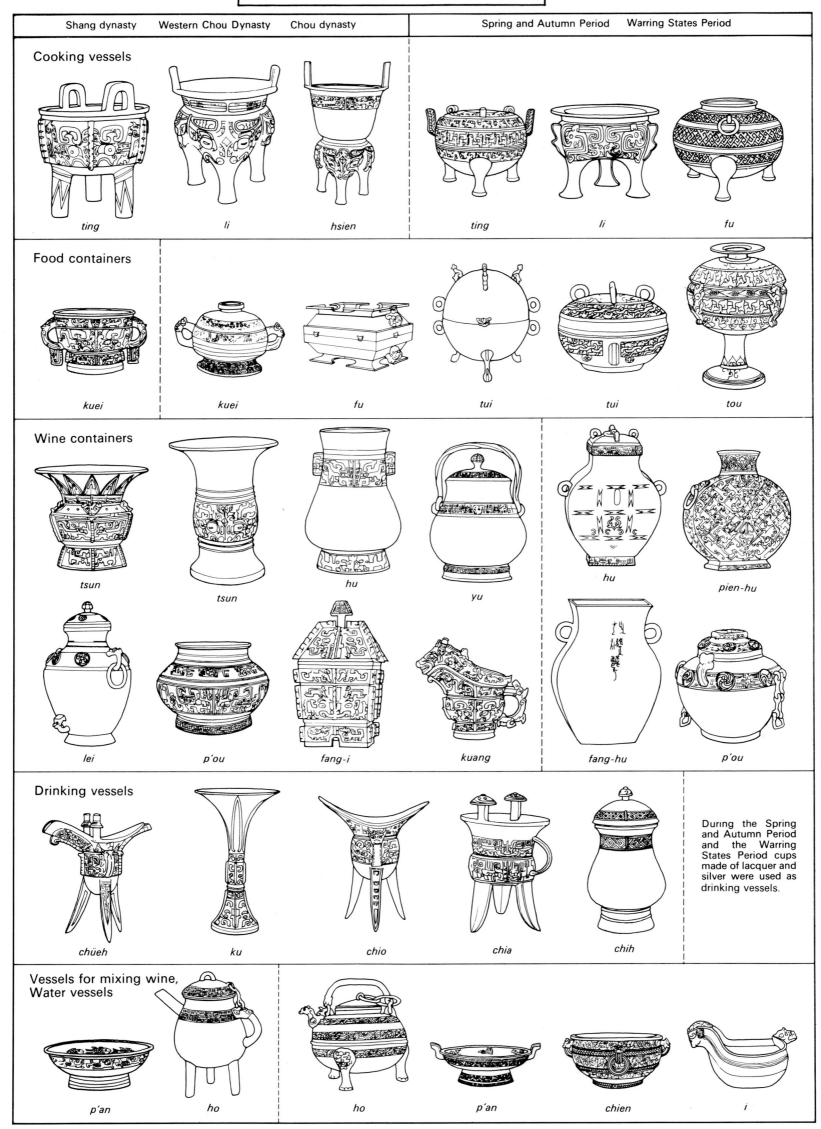

	Shang dynasty	Western Chou Dynasty	Chou dynasty		Spring and Autumn Period	Warring States Period

Cooking vessels

ting · li · hsien · ting · li · fu

Food containers

kuei · kuei · fu · tui · tui · tou

Wine containers

tsun · tsun · hu · yu · hu · pien-hu

lei · p'ou · fang-i · kuang · fang-hu · p'ou

Drinking vessels

chüeh · ku · chio · chia · chih

During the Spring and Autumn Period and the Warring States Period cups made of lacquer and silver were used as drinking vessels.

Vessels for mixing wine, Water vessels

p'an · ho · ho · p'an · chien · i

DISTRIBUTION OF CHINESE KILN SITES

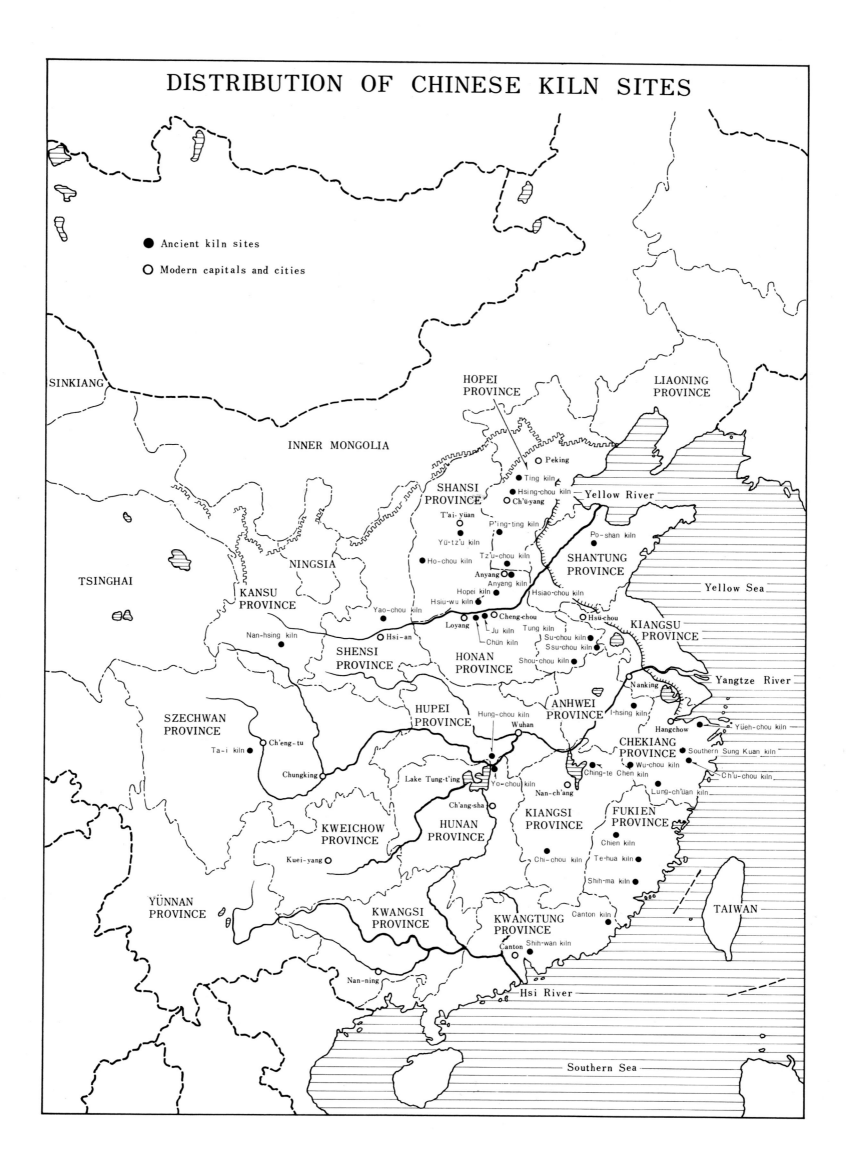

● Ancient kiln sites

○ Modern capitals and cities

SINKIANG

INNER MONGOLIA

HOPEI PROVINCE

LIAONING PROVINCE

NINGSIA

TSINGHAI

KANSU PROVINCE

SHANSI PROVINCE

○ Peking

● Ting kiln

● Hsing-chou kiln

○ Ch'ü-yang

Yellow River

○ T'ai-yüan

● P'ing-ting kiln

● Yü-tz'u kiln

● Po-shan kiln

● Tz'u-chou kiln

SHANTUNG PROVINCE

● Ho-chou kiln

Anyang ○○ ● Anyang kiln

● Hopei kiln

● Hsiao-chou kiln

Yellow Sea

● Hsiu-wu kiln

● Yao-chou kiln

○ Cheng-chou

○ Loyang ● ● Ju kiln

● Tung kiln

○ Hsu-chou

KIANGSU PROVINCE

● Nan-hsing kiln

○ Hsi-an

● Chün kiln

● Su-chou kiln

● Ssu-chou kiln

SHENSI PROVINCE

HONAN PROVINCE

● Shou-chou kiln

Nanking

Yangtze River

SZECHWAN PROVINCE

HUPEI PROVINCE

● Hung-chou kiln

● Wuhan

ANHWEI PROVINCE

● I-hsing kiln

Hangchow

● Yüeh-chou kiln

● Ta-i kiln

○ Ch'eng-tu

CHEKIANG PROVINCE

● Southern Sung Kuan kiln

○ Chungking

Lake Tung-t'ing

● Yo-chou kiln

● Ching-te Chen kiln

● Wu-chou kiln

● Ch'u-chou kiln

● Lung-ch'üan kiln

○ Nan-ch'ang

○ Ch'ang-sha

KIANGSI PROVINCE

FUKIEN PROVINCE

KWEICHOW PROVINCE

HUNAN PROVINCE

● Chien kiln

○ Kuei-yang

● Chi-chou kiln

● Te-hua kiln

● Shih-ma kiln

YÜNNAN PROVINCE

KWANGSI PROVINCE

KWANGTUNG PROVINCE

● Canton kiln

TAIWAN

○ Canton ● Shih-wan kiln

○ Nan-ning

Hsi River

Southern Sea

183

LIST OF PLATES